MW00966246

SELLING
HIGH VALUE
SOFTWARE

Ways to win the deal at the highest attainable value

- *John Coburn* -

Copyright © John Coburn 2005

The right of John Coburn to be identified as the author of this book has been asserted in accordance with the Copyright, Designs and Patents Act 1988.

First published 2005 by John Coburn
Email: info@praxisnow.ie.com

ISBN: 1-4116-5089-1

All Rights Reserved. No part of this publication may be reproduced, stored in a retrieval system or transmitted in any form or by any means, electronic, mechanical, photocopying, recording, scanning or otherwise, except under the terms of the Copyright, Designs and Patents Act 1988 or under the terms of a license issued directly and in writing by the copyright holder and publisher. Such requests should be emailed directly to the publisher at info@praxisnow.ie.

Designations used by companies to distinguish their products are often claimed as trademarks. All brand names and product names used in this book are trade names, service marks, trademarks or registered trademarks of their respective owners.

Discounts on bulk licenses of this book are available to corporations, professional associations and other organizations. For details, please email the publisher or the author directly at info@praxisnow.ie.

For Sean (RIP) and Pauline Coburn.

Table of Contents

Bibliography

Prologue

You have at your fingertips a repository of ideas, observations, strategies and tactics that are designed specifically to help you move up the software solution value chain. The intention is to make a significant and tangible impact on the manner in which you up the ante in your next big-ticket software sales negotiation.

The book is written for entrepreneurs, sales professionals, financiers and senior executives in the software industry. It is based only on real world experiences and has been cleaned of theory. Every part of it can be put into practice in a way that is known to be effective with practical certainty.

The book will take you *inside* the pre-sale *experience* of big ticket contracts. In doing so, it will allow you to share more than twenty years of successes as well as some valuable lessons from the school of hard knocks!

Some of the negotiating ideas, tips and techniques may seem aggressive. Others may not be new to you. Others still, will be subtle. Find the one, two or even ten that you either didn't know about, knew about but had forgotten or knew about but didn't think you could apply. Acting on any one will make a difference.

The book is bottom-line focused. It is written specifically to boost the income you attain from your *existing* software solution. It will also show you some ways to get your customers to fund your future product development. Too good to be true? Read on – because I'm going to deliver on this prospect.

Let's be clear at the outset about what the book is.

- It is a book of ideas to assist your progression up the buyer's value chain. It presents you with a number of ways to maximize your organization's value in making solution proposals, to help you prepare for strategic sales negotiations and to give you some pointers on how you might present your solution.

- It is a record of a multitude of real life experiences from more than twenty years in the global enterprise software industry. It records strategy and counter-strategy in the buyer and seller quest for sustainable, long-term working partnerships.

- It is a "preparatory text" which can get you an extra few steps up the experience ladder before you ever start a big-ticket negotiation!

Let's also be clear about what the book is not.

- It is **not** a book on general negotiation skills. Though it may include some basic negotiation premises, its primary focus is on WHAT the buyer will attempt to negotiate, WHAT you should aim for strategically and HOW you can support your negotiating position.

- It is **not** a complete treatise on software licensing – though it considers many of the most prevalent (and some less prevalent) licensing permutations.

- It is **not** a start-to-finish big-ticket sales process. That doesn't fit into a book! It looks specifically at your position in relation to your readiness to cut deals in the multi-million dollar range, what you should look at in this regard and how you

should articulate that in value terms as part of
your proposal. It then uses the concept of a
Master Services Agreement to get into the
things that make the difference between closing
the deal on one level and closing it at another,
much higher level.

Defining "Big Ticket" and "Mega Ticket" Contracts

For convenience, I am defining a *big ticket* project as an
engagement with a total value of at least three hundred
thousand dollars. Your income stream would typically
consist of a software license (in some form),
maintenance and support services, possibly some
bespoke or tailoring work and perhaps an amount of on-
going professional services including project
management, requirements or functional specification
and so on.

Why "three" hundred thousand dollars? Well, if you sell
all the above for "one" hundred thousand dollars then
you can count yourself in – you've an even bigger win
ahead of you by reading this book! In truth, it is rather
loosely defined. The book is about moving up the value
chain. I personally like the figure "three" because, if
you're selling today for "three", I firmly believe you can
sell tomorrow for more than a million and potentially

several million. And it is entirely within your control to do it.

Also for convenience, I am defining a *mega ticket* project as having a similar structure to a big ticket deal but with a price tag of at least one million dollars. You could generally expect however, that mega ticket deals will run at several million dollars on average.

A Few Assumptions about You

- You either own, sell for or financially control a software company, probably small or medium sized.
- Your company sells enterprise-wide solutions to Corporate, Government or any other potential large-scale users of your software.
- Your solution is of good (not necessarily the best) quality
- You operate in a market where your domain expertise is a significant selling factor.
- You believe that you either have or can get quality people into your team (sales, technical, management)
- Your development, testing, production and delivery processes are up to standard in your industry, and

- You believe you can get more income from your customers.

Just to get You Thinking . . .

A matter that I'm not going to deal with here (but I'm seriously thinking about writing another book on!) is whether the market you are targeting is actually defined correctly! Whether slight or subtle changes to the phraseology or language you use in articulating your value proposition, could radically alter the focus of your business or open up new niche or even super-niche markets for you. Whether relatively small adjustments to your product could bring you into new markets and open new doors. Whether you've been swept along by a tide of "hype" which never actually materialized into a significant market, but left you and your competition stuck in a little pond!

I've been there – and it is so, so difficult to re-invent yourself. The realization that you are there is a major step, although it requires a whole new spurt of entrepreneurship to change things once you've arrived there. But after all, even if you're in sales, aren't you an entrepreneur?

CHAPTER 1

Introduction

A question for you. What have big-ticket software solution buyers from California, Texas, New York, United Kingdom, Germany, Italy, Ireland, Japan, Korea and Australia got in common? Have a think about it.

It's OK – I'll wait . . .

. . . The answer of course is "pain"; they've all got a problem that they want solved and they're willing to pay money to solve it. No big deal there – you got it right – easy! OK, let's try a slightly harder one. Let's assume they all had exactly the same pain. How much money are they willing to pay to solve it? I'll wait a little longer on this one.

. . . take your time.

. . . OK I heard multiple answers that time. So let's look at a few of them.

Answer 1: Depends on what their budget is – what they can afford.

> Yes, but either they can afford to be in the game or they can't. If they're competing on a global stage then they are obliged to play by the global rules. In this case the rule is – be as cost-efficient as possible but don't sacrifice quality of

product or service. If their competitor has the same pain they do, then they're both competing to source a solution as cost-effectively as possible – anywhere on the planet. If one can't afford it, they're out. It's only a mater of time.

Answer 2: Depends on what the solution costs.

See Answer 1.

Answer 3: Exactly the same amount.

Getting there – but not quite! There's a case to say that this is the correct answer. It goes like this. You get a headache – you take a pill. Pain disappears – you're fine now! Until of course the next headache begins – especially if you're out there the night before and the next night and the next night! Of course I'm referring to companies working that bit harder, using their marketing machines that bit smarter, building products that bit better, servicing their customers that bit more. They really need a bigger pill with a longer-lasting, "strategic" effect!

Answer 4: An amount that puts them one or more steps ahead of the competition.

Now you're motoring. For all the above reasons and a lot more besides, especially in big-ticket projects, never ever give a prospect a pill that just takes away their pain. Give them a "bullet" that's not only going to grease their marketing, sales, manufacturing and finance machines, but is going to give them a sustainable, strategic competitive advantage that is so plainly obvious, it jumps out of your proposal.

Amazingly, while this seems obvious, we don't need to do a survey to know that well in excess of 99% of software companies out there are proposing "solutions to pain" plus "how we differentiate against our competition". Very few have set a strategic objective for their sales teams to propose "Curing the cause of *your* pain" plus "how *you* will differentiate against *your* competition". Did you spot the difference?

$300K or $10m?

The difference between a $300,000 and a $10 million dollar deal is not the number of lines of code in the software, or even the size of the team you must assign to the project. Before I tell you what it is, let's look at a few more "is nots". It is not how brilliant your sales presentation was. It is not how old or how new your software is. It is not how well documented your solution is or how well designed it is. It is not even to do with how friendly you are with the CEO of the buying organization and it is not to do with you having zero or poor competition.

The answer is *perceived value*. But the real key is in understanding how that value perception has been created. Clearly all of the above considerations are important, but perceived value is created by a number of factors and you need to consider and have a strategy for every single one of them. They are:

1. A full understanding of the real location and cause of pain

2. An in-depth appreciation for the cost of pain in terms of the existing solution (cost to maintain, recurring costs), the lost opportunity cost (cost of doing nothing) and the strategic "acquired opportunity" for the organization to grow its profits based on your solution.

Just as importantly you also control internal factors in your own company which have a significant bearing on the creation of perceived value. They are:

3. An unswerving belief that your solution is worth more than the pain it resolves (irrespective of the monetary value of that pain)

4. A front-end business-technical sales and executive presence that is capable of representing that belief as well as being capable of understanding the causes and costs of the buyer's pain.

Having the right answers to the list of "is nots" (and more) covered in the first paragraph *support* your created perception of value. Although it could be argued that these factors, combined with your wonderful architecture and the excellence of your development, testing and delivery processes all contribute to the aura of perceived value – which of course, they do, my interest here is in the things that create the *really big value boost*. These are the things that make the difference between hundreds of thousands and millions of dollars. Read them again above; they are listed 1 to 4.

As you read through the book, now that you know *what* creates the *big boost* in perceived value, become aware of *how* you can use these things to create value perception.

Why Your Solution is Worth $5m+

Well, if you've believed what I've said so far, you may be of the view that "My solution is worth $10m because I believe it is and because I know I can articulate its value proposition at that level to my prospect in a way that I know will convince them." If you've got to this stage, fast forward to the end of the book. You have arrived, I can teach you nothing and I will buy and recommend your book to many others.

If you're still here, you may be thinking "The concept stacks up OK. But there is a lot more I would need to know about not only why I should believe my solution is worth millions, but how I can get that idea past the finishing line. How can I actually do the deal at that level"? If that's what you're thinking, you are right on! That's the goal – to teach you how!

Your starting point along this road of course, is that you need a buyer that is capable of transacting at that size. Not every organization can do it. Bear in mind also that if your traditional customers have been buying at a few hundred thousand dollars, it is going to be pretty difficult to get them to up the ante to a few million. Something therefore has to change.

Changes

It is worth looking at the kind of changes that can make a difference here.

One change that could occur is that the problem which your solution solves might have to be expanded or expressed in different terms. Perhaps there is a much bigger win for the customer just one step removed from the immediate problem. If you provide software to a Bank to manage its credit card Call Centre, what would it take to expand it's use right across the Bank for all account holders, all customer service issues etc..

Your main contact could be one step removed from the person or group in your customer's organization that you should really be talking to. That person may be able to take a much bigger decision, make a much bigger commitment, and solve a much bigger problem! For example, if you sell software to a University Department to build on-line learning courses, what would it take to sell the same software University-wide, where all Departments could standardize on it, share course modules and experiences etc... The returns to the customer would be massive!

If you sell software to end users to manage say, their business purchases using commercial credit cards, what if the Bank were to provide your software directly to its customers? What sort of massive branding and resale license could you construct? What unique propositions for the Bank could you build into your software? What would it be worth to them? Who in the bank could make this decision? Why aren't you already talking to them?

Those words "what if" are very useful ones. A worthwhile exercise is to make the analogies to your own business. Use a clean sheet of paper and ask yourself ten "What ifs". The answers will enlighten you!

Whatever the change, it is your decision to initiate and progress it. Not just think it up! But making it happen. Rallying your troops, getting the appointments, proposing the solutions. Beyond the changes, it is down to basic sales prospect qualification. It's entirely up to you to *decide* to target prospects who not only can sustain this level of investment but who have the ability to massively profit from it.

Up The Ante

Prospects and customers – they're intellectual as well as emotional people. They don't always have the authority or budget ownership to do what they would like to do, but they generally understand good business sense. If they are already transacting with you or a competitor at a few hundred thousand, then either they themselves or their team were trusted enough by their company to articulate an internal return on investment, execute a contract with you and put their necks on the line to ensure successful implementation and rollout.

So here's a question for you. Do you think that if you were able to demonstrate to them beyond a shadow of a doubt that their company would make $2 million for an investment of $1 million within six months of rollout and make $3 million per year thereafter for an annual investment of $1 million, that they would say thanks but no thanks? I don't think so. If they did, then you're talking to the wrong person and you should go upstairs immediately. For sure, they may be comfortable in their "safe" jobs and don't want to upset the status quo, or they might not have the time to devote to it immediately. But generally, if you can make the proposition, they'll not only listen but, assuming your relationship is what it should be, they will help you elevate your idea to where it counts.

It is a very good idea to develop a habit of constantly proactively searching for these new horizons. Your profound understanding of your customer's business (you do have it don't you?) is completely wasted unless you are using it to identify these big opportunities. Doing this in a team context, formally and regularly in meetings

- listing, discussing, short-listing, exploring and acting upon good ideas can set you apart from the field and serve your customer like no other.

If There's a Void Between Understandings . . .

Many times, especially in international contracts where markets have evolved independently, the Seller's "frame of reference" is significantly different from the Buyer's frame of reference. By frame of reference, I mean the language, the models, the processes, even many of the technical terms being used are different! It's a real barrier to competing for international contracts. All the more so when you've got to contend with the (thankfully lessening) "not invented here" syndrome. Whether you are an American doing business in France, an Englishman doing business in Germany or an Irishman doing business in the US, the first step in the communication process is establishing a common frame of reference. This is often done informally and without being stated. Nevertheless, both of you are trying to get a fix on the other's frame of reference.

Many times I have discovered during the early stages of a major sale that even apparently minor differences, often process differences, between the way various markets have evolved, have major implications when applied to another market. Not all "models" can be easily lifted of course, but it only takes one great idea to be transported to have a significant implication for the buyer's business. The Banking industry in particular is rife with these differences; it has the Latino, Anglo-Saxon, Islamic, Nordic and many other "banking object models" which software companies have to contend with! And these are only the untouchable ones!

... There's a Gulf Between Expectations

Another question for you - if you truly have a solution to a problem that can save your prospective customer millions of dollars each year, is it reasonable or even good business practice to charge a one-time licensee fee of $500K? I'll wait while you read that again!

... It's not tough really!

Not in my book! What if you were able to develop and fully deploy it for $50,000? It makes no difference. Your license fee should not be linked in any way whatsoever to your costs. It should be linked wholly and solely to your prospect's savings (or earnings) as constrained by the competitive landscape (others offering a similar solution to yours at a certain price).

But hey, you're in the software industry! In this industry we create, innovate, analyze, and react. We build on the back of ideas and our customers' buy-in. So if you are doing this right, the competitive landscape, which will always be there, should have a significantly lesser influence on your selling proposition, because your proposal should stand on its own merits. It is differentiated, it provides outright competitive advantage to your customer and the return on investment it offers is clear and beyond question. If you have initiated a "change" such as some of those mentioned earlier, you are in a very strong position, because you have uncovered a new area that is thus far untouched by your competition and you can command a unique proposition.

Your value proposition either increases income (or whatever metric your prospect's business uses) or reduces costs for your prospect. You set your buyer's pricing expectation here. It is your starting point before any negotiation. But of course, you don't reveal it yet!

The Mincing Machine

When your buyer has completed its initial decision and approval cycle to go forward with your idea, you will be under several different pressures on various fronts – pressure to tangibly demonstrate your idea, to run a trial, to build a "steel thread" process from front-end to back-end, to develop more fully the "vision", and last but not least, commercial pressure.

As soon as your prospect knows that you want full and reasonable payment for your solution (you do, don't you?) despite your brilliant idea, the value you place on it will be under serious downward pressure immediately.

Your prospect will want to undertake a due diligence exercise on you, potentially at a level of detail and rigour that will leave you absolutely floored! Not only can this drag its feet for several months, even a year or more, but the amount of detail you will have to provide on everything from your customer deployments, your internal development process, personal references for you, a complete audit of your application and physical security etc…, will absorb a very significant amount of time both from you and your team. This can be a traumatic process. So traumatic, and almost consistently so in my experience over many projects, I call it the "mincing machine"!

The prospect will put you through this mincing machine before you get close to signing anything. And when you're close, they will mince you again just to make sure that you stay minced!

How does that sound? Nasty? It is! So be ready for it. Know that it's coming. When it's over, know that you only thought it was over because it's coming around again - and this time the mincing machine means business! And when it's finally finished, anything up to two years later (!), you may even be told that there's no deal, that you priced yourself out of it and that it's unlikely you'll be invited back! While there are no guarantees, depending on who said it, it may just mean that you're still being minced and haven't come through the machine yet!

If that sounds like perseverance to you then you understand the situation.

The coming chapters will give you some ideas on how to maximize the value of your solution, how to stand fast in your commercial proposal, how to make it through the mincing machine intact and how to position your company for a wonderful future.

Your Goal – the "Master Software License and Services Agreement"

It can have many titles, but the one that seems most popular is the "Master Services Agreement" (MSA) – an abbreviated form for "Master Software License and Services Agreement". It is a monstrous legal contract, often running at well over a hundred pages. It sets out an umbrella purchase agreement with you which may include any type of products or services that may be specified in any number of "Statement of Work" attachments to it, now or subsequently! It usually specifies an initial purchase commitment and it's only worth doing for big numbers.

Your goal is to get as many of these as your company can *manage*. An interesting dimension to the MSA is that you may have a number of them with different customers, yet despite the fact that your software solution is fundamentally the same, it may be represented very differently in each one. For example, one may be for an outright development license for your software, one may be for a standard use license with no modifications so that your customer can benefit from your future releases and support, or one may be for a completely bespoke solution that you will develop on top of your existing architecture and data model.

Howsoever it is presented; you'll know you have it when it uses the word "Master" on top, when it is clearly structured as an agreement to which future agreements will attach, when it is just your company's name in the vendor section and when you've had to loose a few pints of blood, sweat and tears just to get hold of it!

The Master Services Agreement is truly the "holy grail" of contracts for a software company and it is reserved for only the few who can step up to the mark. This book is substantially about how you can negotiate these agreements, what you should look out for and how you can maximize their value to your company.

CHAPTER 2

Attracting and Finding the Platinum Opportunities

Although I'm not setting out to teach you how to prospect for big fish, it is worth summarising the types of bait that big fish are attracted to. It is also worth looking at some of the dangers of big-game fishing, their tastes and how they like their meals served.

Stay Out of the Jaws

But first, you need to avoid being eaten alive.

Big fish have strong jaw-bones and can snap you into pieces when you're not looking. Really, they can. Here are some ways they can:

- You spend so much time and resource doing your very best to service the big fish that your smaller fish suffer. Your quality of service drops, word spreads and your customers leave. You're out of business.

- You put most or all of your development resource into building new solutions for the big fish that you become almost exclusively dependent on the big fish for continuity of income to sustain your effort. The big fish hic-cups – you're gone.

- You assign your best people to the big fish project, leaving less capable people to develop your "standard product". Your "standard product" finally gets released to your wider customer case, you discover major issues with the new release and you can't roll back. Ouch!

- You invest massive effort in the pre-sale between proposal preparation, travel and subsistence, people's time and your own almost complete absorption into the project. It doesn't close. Six months, a year, eighteen months pass – still not closed. Do you just drop it and do your best to recover the rest of your business or do you keep it going even though you know the only way forward eats 80% of your time. Not a nice decision and a very big risk.

There are many more ways you can get eaten alive and this is your heads-up to deal with it before it gets acute. By knowing some of the dangers in advance, it is hoped that you can navigate a safer path more easily. While each company situation will differ, you should not forget a few of the basics.

- Your existing customers, though they may be smaller, may be the life-blood of your company so stay in touch.

- Don't leave mediocre people responsible for your standard product releases. If necessary, hire new people and mix them with experience both on the big-fish and the standard fish!

- Manage your time. Consider seriously how many big-fish you can realistically play and land at one time without toppling your boat!

- Don't spend all your time between playing with big fish and managing your business. Schedule a percent of your time on continually searching for the creative changes / opportunities discussed earlier.

The Open Sea

It is safe to say that big fish tend to be found more often where:

- The water is deep. Money circulates more freely. Their markets are sustaining ones; often financial services, government, manufacturing, distribution and retail, telecommunications or entertainment.

- A large shoal of smaller fish usually swims in
their wake. You can often tell these smaller fish
by their chattering teeth – they have become
afraid to venture beyond the shadow of their
mother-fish! Do you know any companies or
"consultants" like this? They are the project
"hangers-on"! They are constantly trying to
prop-up their credibility by pretending to know
more that they do!

- Food is abundant. They feed heavily. When
times are good, they have lots of little baby fish
to join the shoal behind. When times are bad,
the shoal behind makes a tasty meal by itself!

- The waters are clear. Their branding stands out
– they are easy for all to see. But if you swim
across their path, be sure to don your full-metal
jacket!

- Lots of competition keeps their muscles
exercised. Their game is about market share
and cash generation. They seek the power to go
anywhere and do anything. Support their
agenda and you can stay in the pond – but don't
think about "growing". Too much of that and
they'll find it that bit harder to get their jaws
around you when they need to!

That's enough about the open sea. You know where to go. What you really want to know now is (1) can you get on the boat, (2) how do you hook these fish, and (3) how do you reel them in?

Get on the Boat

Clearly you must have the prerequisites in place as per the five premises below. Having these in place qualifies you to fish.

The five basic premises are:

1. Your prospective buyer is big enough to achieve a return on a multi-million dollar investment.

2. You care a great deal about your existing customers. Your customers like you! You are honest, are of high integrity and very probably are good *fun* to work with. You would be amazed how important the "fun" thing is – and your customers *will* be contacted by your big fish.

3. You have a *vision*. You are entrepreneurial. Even if you don't own the company, understand its vision – the owner's vision. The vision should

be aligned to an "ambitious reality" that can be expressed in your customer's terms; what its means to your customer's business, how it supports your customer's goals etc... An ambitious reality is a big medium to long term goal that is realistic and attainable from the course your company is presently sailing. Show them that you are sailing it. Walk the walk as well as talk the talk.

4. You have the core team in place who, when you raise the bar, can step up to the new mark. Your people will be a very key part of your unique selling proposition in mega-ticket sales.

5. You have the specification, development, testing, production, delivery and quality assurance processes in place. There is no room on the boat for "unconscious competence". You have to know exactly how you got to where you are. You will be called upon to demonstrate that you know.

Hooking One!

I should emphasize that you cannot replace professional, systematic selling, including a structured prospecting plan and process to deliver your sales pipeline in a consistent and predicable way. But hooking a relatively small number of these big fish might just be possible *outside* of your normal "prospecting" system.

It seems that whilst you can do many things to chase or find it, it is the things you do to *attract* it that always seem to be the most effective. Obvious as they might sound, here are a few things you can do to attract big fish:

- Build your *reputation*. Word of mouth relating to you and your company must include references like – "These are people I can work with", "They've gone way out of their way to help me out", "They've always responded", "They know what they're doing", "They understand my business better that I do", "Don't do anything until you talk to ...", "These guys actually care about how I'm doing. Instead of asking me how I'm getting on with the product, they ask me how my business is progressing and constantly come up with new ideas to make it progress a bit faster!".

- Big fish hear things from other big fish, suppliers, customers, the media. Don't think for a moment that the big fish inside the big fish are not constantly keeping their eyes and ears to the ground to see who is standing out, who is making the moves, who they should be having a business relationship with. It's not the company or person who does it once that they look at. It's the one who keeps doing it.

- Think *big*. It may seem obvious but if you don't come up with a big idea, how can you expect to be paid a lot of money for it? If you think big often enough, you will start to talk big. When you talk big, people around you will be inspired to support you and will gravitate to your boat!

- *Network* intelligently. Go where you know the fish gather – their associations, their clubs and their gatherings. Be seen and heard not in a loud way, but in a humble, yet dare I say, a "stunning" way; talk about your vision, your company, your ambitions and your people. Be *stunning*!

- Hire the *best* people. Good people tend to come up with great ideas and great products. They solve problems faster than average people. They come up with better solutions. They work harder and longer and they produce more! That is why big fish are always willing to invest more in good people than in technology or products.

Good people on your team basically provide a better service to your big fish.

- Become a source of consistent innovation and new *ideas*. You need to understand your prospect's business as if it was your own business. One idea alone will not cut it. You should invest regularly in your own creative thinking skills and your industry knowledge. Become a company and a person that people can turn to as a solver of problems.

- Be *flexible*. Be open enough to enter a meeting with one idea and come out of it having sold a completely different (but bigger) one! Roll with the waves. Be prepared to be inconvenienced and to change tack when you can. *Adapt* to the mind-set of your big fish. Look for big savings, big wins.

Here, I've given you just a few ideas for hooking your fish. How big you make the main course and how effectively you reel in these big fish is covered in the following chapters.

Early signs that you may have hooked a hungry big one!

It is important to recognize that not only have you hooked a big fish but that it is ready for your main course! The earlier you can ascertain this, the sooner your life will become more interesting!

Here are a few signs to look for as you examine the fish you've hooked. These indicate how hungry your fish is and just how far and how hard it is prepared to fight before it becomes your main course:

- You find out that your competitors are one or more of the big I.T. / Management Consultancy firms or one or more of the major I.T. Solution providers. Whilst discovering that you are competing with a player in this category can be bad news because you know you're up against high quality competition, it is for the most part, in my opinion, good news.

  It is good news for many reasons and here are just a few:

  i. These companies don't promote price as a basis to do business. This is not to say that they don't discount when forced to. They only discount as a last resort. They tend to transact high and deliver high. Quite apart from the appropriateness or otherwise of their solutions, big fish are generally (but not always) more amenable to placing extra-big ticket contracts on these companies because of a perceived lower risk. If it all goes horribly wrong, the big fish can sue the supplier knowing that the supplier has the funds to meet the potential liability! I should add that such an instance is a rare occurrence.

ii. Most of these companies use third party solutions as the core of their offering. You therefore compete against them by offering direct access to your design and development team without a third party "being in the way"! This lets you react sooner and be far more responsive to your customer's needs. It also conveys first-hand in-depth knowledge of your domain. Most big fish consider this significant. It is your job to make sure they do.

iii. Often, you will find that your competitor is promoting / pushing a proprietary infrastructure on which to house their proposed solutions. While these may be fine products, they are not necessarily the best infrastructure in all circumstances and may place future constraints on your customer's options going forward.

iv. If you are operating in a specialist, niche market, there is a high probability that your domain expertise will exceed theirs by a distance. Have your big fish sign a non-disclosure agreement and present your vision of *their* future.

So if you've found out that this is the nature of your competition, it is reasonable for you to make a good guess that the Big Fish has the type of money you're after to spend on this project.

- The CEO or Senior Executive has taken a personal interest in the project. For example, you are told that he or she has requested weekly or monthly reports on specific progress in the project from the Program Manager or whoever is managing the project. This is a great sign! It means that there are big stakes involved. You've got to uncover these stakes, know exactly what the metrics are, and of course, position your solution accordingly.

- You discover that the cost of annually maintaining the existing solution is massive; it may be housed in giant-sized server farms, it may not be scalable to increasing demands, the original developers may no longer be available etc... This is yet another sign that the stakes are high, that the big fish is likely to be loosing competitive ground in the marketplace and that the project is unlikely to be shelved after whatever process they go through to select a solution.

- The big fish only discovers your bait at the eleventh hour; you saw it just as it was about to take a big bite out of another bait, then you saw it slowly turn away and head for yours. At this stage, it just wants to check yours out to make sure that little grain of uncertainty it had was nothing to worry about. "*Uncertainty*". A shadow of a doubt. You need to hone it on it immediately. You've got to make sure they know that their gut instinct was right and give them the rationale *they were looking for*!

You've now examined the big fish. It looks like its hungry and seems to be well on the hook. At worst, you've got a shot at proposing your solution. At best, the prospect already has a good idea that you will at least make the short list.

Strip-Lining

The Sandler Sales Institute has a useful sales technique which can be used in any number of circumstances. One of the circumstances in which I use it is to test the "verve" of a hooked fish. The technique is known as "negative reverse selling" and it involves "strip-lining" which is another fishing term. Strip-lining means to let some line out to make sure the fish has got a good, unobstructed bite on the bait.

To strip-line is to pull-back a bit from the prospect – move away slightly, becoming somewhat less enthusiastic than the fish. This means that, when the time is right, to actually become more negative than the fish which may seem like the opposite of what you should be doing! A simple example could be:

Prospect: "You mean to say that your solution can actually do this thing?"

You: "Hold on a second. I think I missed something here. I only explained that function as an incidental. What did I miss? Are you saying you would actually use this?"

What you did not do was continue with your pitch on how brilliant your solution was. Instead, you pulled back, and let the prospect continue to sell themselves on it.

In fishing terms, if you felt a nibble at the bait, instead of reeling in quickly to drive home the hook (which it won't), you let out some line so that the fish thinks it OK to swallow! If the fish comes back towards it, it bites, you know the hook is in and you let it play itself!

CHAPTER 3

Review of Software Licensing Options and Permutations

Although not an exact science, the licensing model you choose for your software has a major influence on the degree of success you are likely to attain. Some licensing models do not easily translate to the large scale and some translate very well. The purpose of this relatively short chapter is to review some of the various licensing models available and to look at their suitability to large scale engagements.

In big or mega ticket projects, what you make on your license should be straight gross margin. This of course presumes that you do not "bundle" into the license, services for which you could otherwise charge.

It is amazing just how many non-software organizations still struggle with this! Many companies do not believe that you should be making enormous gross margin on your software because it costs you nothing to produce. That they are paying you separately to deploy it can even be another bone of contention! Consideration is not always given to the scale of the development effort or the entrepreneurial risk that was taken to commit to the development in the first place.

Playing with Fees

What percentage of your overall engagement should be occupied by your license fee is really a function of strategy. In services oriented organizations, it is not unusual to see much of, or even the entire software license fee absorbed into volume services contracts. In software product oriented organizations on the other hand, it is relatively rare to see any inclusions whatsoever in the license fee. Product-oriented organizations however seem to be relatively more willing to negotiate on their service fees.

In big ticket project opportunities, it is not at all unusual to see both types of organization competing with each other. With a shrewd buyer, it is not always obvious that a given vendor is playing a strategy of value exchange between services and license fee, and this can be quite difficult to deal with. The only thing you can do is to continue selling your own solutions on its own merits – until you get to the negotiating table. If there is a strategy being played, the buyer knows it and will not exclude you until they have leveraged it. That usually happens sometime between draft contracts being issued and your final negotiating round!

Application Service Provision (ASP)

ASP or centrally hosted, web-based application delivery went through a series of ups and downs since it was discovered in the mid nineties. Initially, it was "hyped" as the only viable service delivery model for the twenty first century. A couple of years later it was in the doldrums. Companies had bad experiences with issues such as performance, security, poor management tools, and continuity of business. Then, over time, most or all of these issues got resolved.

Coupled with massive bandwidth improvements and widespread availability of better communications infrastructure, ASP is now very much in vogue once more. Today, there are very few who would doubt the potential of ASP as a delivery vehicle for both consumer and business applications requiring massive scalability.

Most major commercial and government organizations now have web-based consumer and business access to their services. Whether hosted in private data centres or using external managed service centres, consumer confidence in these internet services has somewhat improved. Although there is still a way to go before the mass market will trust the internet as a secure transactional channel, most service providers offer it as just one of many available channels.

Bottom line – it's big, and you need to consider it if you're not already doing it.

Transaction Fee Model

With the ASP delivery model, came new ways for the software industry to license its solutions in transaction-based applications. Although not always taken up, indeed often veered away from, transaction-based licensing permutations are now practical.

Because both consumer and business applications can now be centrally administered, the opportunity to track or audit individual transactions in different ways without impacting security is viable. Instead of procuring a license in whatever manner previously existed, the opportunity now exists to pay for the software based on the volume of transactions passing through the service.

Transaction throughput is an accurate measure of the actual success or failure of many application services. Because of this, the opportunity exists for both buyer and seller to absorb part of or even the entire license fee into a fee per transaction.

Where appropriate, this allows the risk of success or otherwise to be shared. It allows the software vendor to put "skin in the game".

Transaction Definitions and Fee Permutations

The licensing model described is relevant to more than purely financial transaction systems.

Financial Transaction Fee Models

Clearly, a financial transaction can be tracked and audited. A fee can be charged on the basis of either the number of transactions irrespective of transaction size, the accumulated value of transactions within a given period or the absolute value of transactions. The absolute value of transactions is calculated based on the total accumulated value less any transactions that were credited back or reimbursed. For example a travel agent may have recorded a customer purchase of five airline tickets but since only four travelled on the day, the fifth ticket fee was reimbursed.

Business Process Transaction Models

With well architected software, it is also possible to track each time a particular business process in invoked. For example, in retail banking, business processes may include *order check book, cancel credit card, check balance* etc... This is an especially interesting licensing model where multiple channels have access to a central repository of business processes that can be reused. For example a check book may be ordered not only over the internet, but also by 'phone via a call centre, in a branch, from an ATM and so on.

The idea of being able to charge a fee each time a business process in invoked hugely expands the possibilities and scope for transaction fee licensing and, with the right application architecture, is very well suited to large scale projects.

In general, transaction fee based licensing is not very popular. The reasons for this would seem to be:

- Reluctance on the part of the service provider to reveal its business volume to an external party.

- An unwillingness to share a potentially lucrative upside with the solution vendor.

- Reluctance to allow any monitoring or measurement of any of its corporate activities

Despite this, transaction fee based licensing models can be reliably implemented without the need for specific, confidential or associated personal details. It is a viable licensing method.

It is worth noting that many financial institutions themselves use their internal cost per transaction as a measure of their own performance. Whilst the formulae that drive these measurements are usually confidential, your articulation of costs in the form of a transaction fee is actually a very interesting measure for them.

In some cases, even though they may not ultimately agree a transaction fee based model with you, it will set a meaningful expectation of your value position. They are quite likely to combine your complete, inclusive costs over three to five years, divide by the total number of forecasted transactions within that period and compare it to an internal cost per transaction target.

With these type of prospects, you should try to uncover what their cost per transaction target actually is and over what period of time. Get this and you are well on the road to creating value.

Recurring Nature

A key advantage of licensing based on a transaction fee is its non-ending, recurring nature. Although upper limits are sometimes agreed, the count typically recommences on the license anniversary date. Here again, service providers often struggle to understand why you should be paid annually in this way! When all or part of your prospect's issue with this, is the actual amount of money they must pay being the same each year, there is another permutation you might consider. This is a reducing transaction fee based on specific volume milestones being met. For example, the fee per transaction for the first twenty million transactions may be $0.18, for the next ten million it may be $0.12 and thereafter it may be $0.06. It may take two years or ten years to reach the lower rate but it is nevertheless a viable alternative.

Development License

A development license is a regular feature in big ticket software projects. It infers full source code and documentation access to part or all of your software. It also authorizes your prospect to completely re-brand and modify the code as it deems appropriate.

There are a few subtleties that you may be able to *work in* to your license conditions as your fee negotiation progresses. You may be better positioned to leverage some of them if you defer their negotiation until actual exchanges take place. In other words, when you are being "minced" on the license fee, offer to trade concessions.

"Powered by . . ."

If your prospect's intention is to ultimately develop the application for use by consumers or an end user business community, try to get recognition on the end user screen. For example, a small "Powered by [your company]" icon on one corner of the screen and / or recognition on the end user's log-on screen can tangibly benefit you. This will at least get you some value in the wider marketplace if not immediate income.

Co-development and Support

Since it is your prospect's intention to modify the code directly, you may be able to build a case whereby you actually co-develop the new code with your prospect. A significant incentive for your prospect to discuss this possibility is that if you are fully up to date on the code modifications made, you would be capable of providing support services that would otherwise be exclusively internal to your prospect. If you can negotiate this, you not only have development services opportunities available to you, but on-going support services as well. There will almost always be two camps in your prospect's organization; those who firmly believe that applications should be solely supported in house (usually to preserve competitive advantage), and those who favour outsourcing (usually driven by economics). So choose the recipient of your proposal carefully.

Licensing Restrictions

Restrictions on sub-licensing are often used to reduce the sometimes significant risks associated with development licenses. It may be your prospect's intention to develop a solution that it will directly sell to a wider market, perhaps even potentially in competition with you. You might have considered this in the context of your prospect's geographic market being one that you either could not or would not target yourself directly. Here, you need to prevent your prospect from sub-licensing the final solution outside of its territory to other parties who could potentially compete with you on your own turf. If your solution is modular or component-based, you may restrict your license to specified components only.

In general though, it is true to say that if a prospect is going to pay a lot of money for a development license, it will expect no restrictions whatsoever. But when you think about it, that's exactly what you want them to think – "pay a lot of money – no restrictions"!

Rights to Intellectual Property

In some cases, you may be able to negotiate either full intellectual property rights or at least resale rights for your prospect's finally developed solution in your own market. This is not always valuable, but there are occasions when you can acquire a major asset as a direct result of this apparently simple trade.

Development licenses are for obvious reasons higher value licenses than other forms of licensing. They also demand that your software is of an appropriate state that an external party can readily follow its documentation from requirements definition through functional specification, business use case definition, architecture, data model, schemas and right through to code listings.

If you're like most other software companies, you may have some clean-up work to do before you can get value for it. Bear in mind that the clean-up work can sometimes be significant.

Licenses Based on Registered Users, Concurrency or CPU

There has been a shift over the last ten years away from perpetual licensing models and toward annually recurring licensing. For the end user, the up-front cost is reduced. For the software vendor, it provides a lucrative recurring income stream. Whereas previously, the only recurring element of the software project was annual maintenance and support, the move to a recurring income model has actually served to highlight and enforce the life-time value of customers. Before, big one-time payments plus modest annual support fees ran the risk of the software vendor's attention being focused elsewhere as new big on-time opportunities arose. Now, an on-going medium sized annual income streams keeps the focus on maintaining value!

Annually recurring fee income based on registered users is one of the most popular licensing methods used in the software industry currently. Although most prevalent in small and medium ticket projects, it is also used in big ticket engagements.

Some of the traditional licensing models being widely used include:

Registered Users

A registered user license is one where the licensee can license the software for use by up to a maximum number of individual users. Although the purchased license may be perpetual, the modern method is to license annually with account being taken of changes in user numbers. An example where user numbers can change substantially in a short space of time is commercial credit cards, where browser access to statements, expense reports or management information is required as programs roll out.

Concurrency

Concurrent user licensing is where a declared or enabled maximum number of users may be simultaneously logged into the application. Concurrency is an older form of licensing and is relatively unsuited to big ticket projects.

CPU based licensing

CPU based licensing is still used by many of the big database, middleware and system software providers. Basically, it sets the license price in accordance with the number and power of CPUs on which it sits. Often a factor when pricing solutions requiring database and middleware engines, the cost can become significant in an overall solution context.

Although far from exhaustive, the licensing options listed
is this chapter suggest that your objectives are best
served by remaining flexible as big ticket opportunities
are presented. Often, during your early stage
information collection and probing of your prospect, a
particular licensing permutation will stand out.

A wider commercial strategy designed around one
permutation may contrast very significantly with that
designed around another. Consider therefore that your
choice of licensing model is a strategic determinant of
your overall plan to close these opportunities at their
maximum attainable value.

CHAPTER 4

The Master Software Licensing and Services Agreement (MSA)

Gallons (or litres) of blood, sweat and tears will be shed during your quest to sign these hefty legal agreements with your prospects. There will be several times when you will be tempted even to walk away and say "it's not worth it". Actually, depending on what sort of person you are, that might be the very best thing you could do!

This book is written for those who are willing to persevere, knowing that it could take up to two years or even more to conclude a MSA. Some of course, can be concluded in nine months. I've never experienced one that took less than six months. The two year plus scenario is usually the result of political turmoil in high places within the prospect organization and I'll be talking more about that later. I do not believe that any prospect would intentionally take two years or more before even starting a project. Nevertheless, it is a regular occurrence which we suppliers just have to accept.

A very frustrating thing about long drawn out contracts is that, during the two plus years they may take, there will be several occasions when finally signing it seems imminent! Just when you think you're finally there, something happens to scupper it.

If you're a small or medium sized company, opportunities like these tend to get discussed around the board table. So when you think you're just about there, do your career a favour and stay objective and less than over-enthusiastic at the board table.

So what actually are MSA's?

As the introduction to the book stated, they can be called many things, but fundamentally they are legal agreements put in place to enable the on-going supply of products and services to the buyer. Obviously, as I am not a Lawyer, it is not my intention to undertake a forensic, legal analysis of an agreement. I do intend however, to undertake a commercial or business analysis of a typical agreement; the "dance" that is typically had between you and your buyer as you are building your agreement, the contentious issues which arise most often, and the negotiating position you might adopt to support your engagement.

Why Use an MSA?

This is actually a better question that you might first think. After all, there are many different types of legal "instruments" available such as a plain old Software License Agreement, a Professional Services Agreement, a Project Agreement or any number of other Agreements. A MSA has a few differences:

- It "allows" for on-going flexibility in relation to what actual work or service is being placed on you, the vendor.

- It enables the buyer to fully vet your company for policy conformance, standards compliance and any other pre-requisite requirements, once only. This means that a standard "process" does not have to be repeated each time a piece of work is required.

- It confers "preferred supplier" status on your company. You have not only been vetted, but you have agreed to supply your products and services at preferential rates to the buyer and under special conditions.

There are a number of other things that sets a MSA apart from other agreements and I'll go into them over the coming chapters.

Mission Critical

A key implication of successfully concluding a MSA is recognition of your company as a "strategic" supplier. The term "strategic" here usually means that your technology or service is considered *mission-critical* to the overall project initiative. The implications of being mission-critical are obviously significant. Because you are mission-critical, the need is emphasized on the buyer's side to tie you down on many fronts in the MSA. A very good reason for this is so that you won't be able to exploit your position after the buyer has committed beyond the point of no return. Examples of areas where you will typically be tied down on include:

- License fees
- License structure and authorization
- Your rate sheet (daily rates and subsistence)
- The people you assign to the project
- Ownership of intellectual property

. . . and so on.

Before the Dance

Just before I get into the dance you will be doing with your big-ticket prospect, let's take a moment to summarize where you're at.

- You made a decision with conviction to up the ante, to move up the value chain and to proactively prepare for and attract projects in the multi-million dollar range.

- You examined your company, your own beliefs, your customer base, your served markets, your products, services and technology to come up with some fresh ideas on how to create more value. And you came up with more than a few!

- You headed for the coast to see if you could get on the boat that fishes for big game and discovered that they were expecting you, wondered why it took you so long and had your seat and rod waiting for you. Actually you didn't even know that you owned a rod – you were going to hire one. Yet there it was – your name engraved on it. It even seemed familiar!

- You set out on the boat looking for a big fat Tuna. But one of the other fishermen just happened to mention to you in passing that Great White Sharks and even some Whales also eat the type of bait that you're fishing with! You've no other bait with you, so you decide just to fish.

- You get a bit frustrated because, now that you're in the boat, you see all the other fishermen casting, hooking and netting, yet you don't seem to be able to catch anything. But they're nice guys and you're inquisitive – you ask and they give you answers. Initially, you don't really understand all the answers but you talk the talk and walk the walk nevertheless.

- After several casts, you finally felt a major tug on your bait, but instead of reeling it in fast, you stripped some line, let whatever it was bite right into the bait.

The water is very clear. So clear in fact that you get a brief glimpse of a shadow - a chance to examine just for a moment what you've hooked even though it's still quite a distance away. It's an absolute giant! You've hooked something really, really big!

Now what do you do?

Start the Dance

Now you do all the things that a good solution salesperson or entrepreneur does best. You build your relationships. You learn the buyer's organization. You discover all of the various pains, their causes and their relative perceived value. You understand what is driving that value. You find out who holds which strings. You press the flesh again and again. You build trust. You find out who is actually experiencing which pains. You discover the competition. You identify your strengths and opportunities as they apply to the buyer organization. You build perceived value for your solution and your people. Then you build more perceived value. After that you build even more perceived value.

Before you arrive at the last "routine" in your dance – the negotiation, it is worth mentioning some of the actions and interactions that may take place during your long nine month to two year dance. There will be many proactive and reactive events, deliverables and preparation that will be occupying your time as you do all of the things in the previous paragraph. Some of them you will control. Others, your prospect will firmly control. Some will be very uncomfortable! Some will be a piece of cake!

As you progress your opportunity, remember that you will be commencing your communication with your big fish in, potentially, a completely "green field" context; they may know very little about you. Their frame of reference may be totally different to yours.

If you are using a selling system such as Strategic Selling, Consultative Selling, the Sandler Selling System or Dale Carnegie's System, the sequence and timing of these actions will be carefully controlled. In this book, I'm not worried about how you do it. It is my intention only to highlight these events in your process because you'll be doing them time and time again. How well you do them is for another book. I'm consciously trying to avoid using the term "steps" in your dance, because they are not actually "steps" which always take place in a set sequence. They are more "events", because they are not in chronological order and some may not necessarily be part of your particular engagement at all!

So, here are a few of the events and deliverables that may occupy your time over a typical nine month to two year plus timescale.

The Initial, Exploratory Call

This is the one where you finally get to talk to the person "holding the baby" in the prospect's organization. He or she may even have called you.

Objective

To *grab attention just enough to get to the next stage.* This could involve them sending you an RFP document, giving you an appointment, or agreeing with you some electronic meeting format that might involve a larger number of people without obliging you, at this stage, to incur the time and costs of travelling. Of course I don't need to say – *don't fire all your bullets* in this first round! You'll be needing new ammunition at almost every step in the process.

Your First Electronic Group Meeting

As you're in the software industry you already know about the wonderful technologies that are now available to let you have group audio conferences accompanied by web-enabled presentations, white-boarding, and live sharing of applications from anywhere on the globe. If you're not familiar with these incredibly useful and now indispensable tools, you can check them out at http://www.webex.com or http://main.placeware.com.

This is where you will attempt to capture the attention of the group by (a) articulating your experience, your vision, your technology, (b) showing them something that proves you know what you are talking about and last but definitely not least, (c) probing into the next level of detail on your prospects needs

Objective

At this stage, your objective is to get the prospect's agreement to send you the Request for Proposal (RFP), or sometimes called an Invitation To Tender (ITT), if one exists. If it doesn't, then you should aim to get in front of the prospect and help them get down into the detail – a great opportunity for you to positively influence the requirements in both your own and your prospect's favour.

Your RFP Response

In many cases, especially where a complex, potentially multi-million dollar solution is being sought, the RFP will include form after form of "fill-in-the-blank" type templates. In particular, a comprehensive set of individual requirements may be presented and you may be asked to score each one as have, will have (planned), can have (if paid), cannot have (considered not viable – propose an alternative way it might be done), or do but do differently. Your prospect will expect your reply to be presented exactly as they've requested it – all forms filled out, present and complete.

Objective

The objective now is to stand out from the crowd. Follow a few simple rules – (1) Use someone who can write to excite while remaining within the realms of truth and *reasonable* license. Write in terms of how the customer benefits, not how brilliant or clever you are, (2) Even though it wasn't asked for, write an "Executive Summary" – a five to ten page quick read of your entire proposal. When you send your response by email, you will be sending several individual documents – your executive summary, the main proposal body requested and the individual attachments that have been requested. If you do it right, they will love you for your Executive Summary! (3) They may have requested two copies. Send four professionally bound copies by courier. Each one must look good and feel good in the hand! This is actually far more important that you might think! (4) Follow-up with 'phone calls to confirm that they've received it, follow-up with calls to get initial reactions from various parties, follow-up with calls to organize a formal presentation meeting. Keep asking about next steps in the process. Stay engaged.

I.T. / Technical team Contacts

Expect many group conference calls, several group meeting, lots of frustration and truck loads of pressure to produce and deliver before you ever get the sale!

Objective

Recognize that you are being audited at every step. Your objective must be (1) to comply with the prospect's core policies and procedures, (2) to demonstrate the formality and structured nature of your company's internal processes, (3) to prove your team's competency, and (4) to demonstrate that their people can work well with your people.

Deliverables

Over the course of time you could be expected to deliver full documentation on your disaster recovery plan, your development, testing, production and quality assurance processes, your deployment documentation, your security, compliance and health and safety policies, technical specifications and more.

Cautions

There are traps here. Obey a few basic rules and you'll make it through. The rules are (1) don't release your detailed architecture design or data model– it is your intellectual property and state this when asked (you will be asked!). It is fine to release the "overview" only. (2) Don't volunteer information you weren't asked for, (3) Never allow any paper or electronic documentation to go to the prospect until it has been reviewed by at least one other senior person on your project team, (4) "Assert" your position as an authority on your subject. Don't loose sight of the fact that you are the subject matter expert even if they've got the title. Just because their organization is bigger than yours does not mean that an individual's opinion is better than yours. But be careful – don't talk down and remain humble, and (5) Look for weaknesses in your company's processes, documentation, specifications, procedures, security compliance etc… that you can pre-empt before it becomes an issue.

Business Team Contacts

These contacts are great opportunities to engage in a two-way learning process about each other's perspectives and ideas. Whilst these engagements will continue well after the contract is negotiated, what is being looked at here is not only to identify the gap between what you have and what is required, but how well you engage, how quickly your team and their team can cut to the chase, how well they communicate, the rapport that exists, how willing your company is to openly discuss the hows and wherefores (under signed non-disclosure agreement of course).

Objective

Your core objective here is to *build maximum value* for your solution. Other objectives which should sit comfortably with this are to ascertain the percentage fit of what you have and *will have* (more on this later) against the overall requirements, determine both the *viability* and level of *effort* to build new custom components of the requirement and to build up a picture of how their project organization works.

Deliverables

As time progresses, you can expect to be preparing outline requirements and even some functional or business use-case definitions. A big deliverable here will be your team's performance during regular conference calls. This includes leadership, focus, understanding, communication, organization, team alignment and follow-up.

Cautions

Adopt each of the same cautions listed under the I.T. team above. Add these – (1) If it seems that they're spending their quota of good will for reasonable consultancy (in your opinion) without paying for it, put it on a commercial footing. Propose an amount of money to be used as a pool for pre-contract consulting engagement. The business team may not love this idea but they'll understand your need for it and you should expect them to be amenable to negotiating it. (2) Don't prematurely engage the project! If you get to the point of thinking that the work being carried out between the two teams is getting too detailed or comprehensive, use your senior level influence to stand up and say "Hey, let's not do this now. This is full project engagement. What do we need to do to help you move forward from here without tying my team up when we don't even have a contract yet?" They'll value you more for it!

Project Team Contacts

These contacts are an amalgamation of the business and technical teams, often including also an executive presence from each side. They will become more regular in the later stages of your pre-sale dance as you and your prospect attempt to hone in on the make-up and structure of the project team, roles and assignments.

Objective

Your objective here is to remain professional and focused on the agreement being signed before you can fully engage. However, it is also your objective to position key people on your team into senior, strategic roles in the prospect's project team. I include here any role right up to and including Project Director, either alone or on behalf of your prospect, or as joint Project Director.

Deliverables

You will be expected to provide lists and backgrounds of key people you would propose to be part of the project team. You will be asked to make proposals of who should do what from your side. If not, proactively make them. Be forward-thinking and ambitious in the amount of resource and seniority of resource you can make available.

Cautions

(1) Give credit where credit is due (in front of the Senior Executive), take credit when it is given, but be very careful indeed of prospect-side individuals who publicly take credit (blatantly in

front of you!) for something that you or one of your team members proposed or suggested. He or she is doing it because they feel they need to. Rather than raise it, probe behind the scenes to see if you can find out why they felt they need it. You might be surprised at what you find! (2) Don't be pushed into exclusively junior or semi-senior roles in the project. Build value for your people – negotiate them into leadership roles in the project, get them the authority they will need to, when necessary, cause some waves in the prospect's organization. Avoid being a post-engagement "lamb to the slaughter" if someone else makes a bad decision. Claim accountability for and be confident in your own team's ability to make decisions and assert your know-how on the project from a vantage point that allows you to deliver success.

Executive One-to-Ones and closed group meetings

These will sometimes be 'phone calls and sometimes face-to-face meetings. Get as many of them as you can. They are superb opportunities to build strong relationships, establish trust and build bridges which can be crossed whenever a problem arises. Your relationship with the senior executive is the one on which the sale will be made. It is also the one that will drive you through to completion post-sale – even through the tornados that invariably arise!

Objective

Bond and build rapport. Engender trust through honesty, integrity and an unswerving belief in your ability to serve your prospect in ways that you haven't even thought of yet. Nothing else.

Deliverables

A working, approachable and genuine relationship. They've already heard all about you from their colleagues and they respect their opinions. Now they want to see you in the flesh, get to know you a bit better and very probably want you to leave each meeting you have with them with this one message:

> *"Succeed in this project, demonstrate that you are the best as we think you are and you will be very well rewarded. There is an unlimited supply of additional projects for you in our organization and your success in this one is your ticket to the next show.*

However, fail in this project and I will personally see to it that you're finished in this industry. If I can take the shirt off your back, I will, and I will do everything that I can do to see that you never get back onto this business".

They'll never say that of course!

Cautions

Just be honest, humble, appreciative, have a bit of fun and don't slip up! Oh, and be successful in the project no matter what it takes.

You don't really get this amount of pressure in the small and medium sized deals do you? I think it is reasonable that you should be paid more – don't you?

Due Diligence Related Contacts

I've separated these contacts from the Project and Technical team meetings even though common personnel will be used. If you're a small or medium sized company, a comprehensive and sometimes gruelling process of due diligence will involve a financial assessment of your company which will look at the probability of your survival long enough to deliver on the project and beyond, and a dependency assessment to see how reliant on this contract you would be. A product and service quality assessment will also be carried out. Some and maybe many of your existing customers will be contacted for references – some will actually be visited, others will be asked to take 'phone calls that can last for more than an hour.

Objective

Know your inner circle of at least your top ten customers who you can rely on to be credible references – even if not on the mega-scale. Explain to them confidentially and personally what you are doing and ask for their help. But also ask them to be honest. By asking them in this way, they will give you generally excellent references, assuming you deserve them (!), mixed with one or two "less than perfects" which will add to credibility and will be very much relegated to second place when probed!

Deliverables

Financial reports, audited accounts, customer contact names, telephone numbers and schedule of meetings and calls as appropriate.

Caution

You might not be that proud of your historical
audited or financial accounts. If not, arrange a
conference call with your Chairman and
Financial Director *before* sending the said
accounts. This can soften any bad news that
might be visible in your accounts and reassure
your prospect of the go-forward condition of the
company.

Purchasing Team Contacts

These people are often professional "hard-ballers". You
can safely assume that they are brilliant at what they do
– after all, they are entrusted with the purse of a big fish.
They know that *literally millions of dollars can be saved
or earned in a single moment of good negotiation*. That
single moment for them could mean the time your heart
skipped two beats when they got up to walk away. It
could be the moment your facial expression changed
when they physically laughed at you after talking about
your license fee. It could be the moment when you
reacted to the suggestion that they wanted equity in
your business if they're going to place this contract on
you. Or it could be the moment you agreed to a license
refund if you didn't fully meet their requirements!

Objective

Stand fast. Don't feel obliged to break down every last detail of your financial proposal. Keep the focus on how much they're about to save even after they pay you the $10m license fee. Put a stake in the ground. If they must laugh, let them laugh and get it over with. If they must react in a particular way, let them. You now have a starting point. Your shot now – if they're going to save $20m exclusively because of you, how do they justify not paying you the amount you've asked? I'm not going to get into the negotiation just yet. That's just a teaser for what's coming later in the book!

Deliverables

This really is the pre-negotiation dance. Each of you are just testing the other for potential "differences in thinking", looking for signs of potential weakness, testing the "verve" of the other. The deliverable at this stage might be a draft "term sheet" which simply outlines the starting position of both parties on each element of the draft Master contract.

Cautions

Millions of them – too many to list! Just concede nothing at this point. Be assertive and steadfast, but do indicate your willingness to discuss counter-proposals in an actual Agreement context. You're not looking for solutions to differences of opinions yet. All you're doing here is understanding the starting point of the other party.

From your first encounter, over time, you will progress to a point where your big prospect desperately wants to do business with you (even if they may not admit it until after they've signed the agreement). They accept you as very probably the single highest industry authority that they would most like to have on their side. Your prospect would pay you a lot of money if they thought you would leave your existing company and join them instead – but of course they also know that they would be shooting themselves in the foot if you did! You have established a significant degree of trust. Your solution is now supported with full, yet realistic credibility.

The prospect sees your people as the best team on the planet – they flourish with new ideas, understand the prospect's business extremely well, are professional, yet personal, in every interaction that takes place. And they are fun to work with. There were great dinners out, drinks shared, flights missed, embarrassing moments, and serious moments. The following morning, your people were always the first to arrive at the office, gave excellent presentations, explained things clearly, questioned the prospect when they were unsure and worked into the evening when required to do so.

You, your team, your company and your solution should be *oozing* with credibility. You may still however be miles away from striking distance!

The "Great Depression"

Thankfully, this may not happen to you, but since I do not believe that I am so unique that I alone have experienced this on several occasions, I'm operating on the basis that it happens not infrequently out there! It has to do with the gaping political gulf that exists in many (all?) large organizations between their I.T. Departments and their Business Departments.

A natural conflict has always existed here. It has to do with the Business team being charged with meeting and exceeding customer demands and growing the business at the fastest achievable pace. The I.T. function on the other hand has to do its best to keep up with an ever growing list of project demands to support the business. When new business requirements end up being entered lower and lower on the priority list, the I.T. Department becomes less and less popular. The natural conflict is compounded by the fact that even previously submitted requirements from the business team often change and are revised, putting increased, often short notice pressure on the I.T. team to deliver even more.

But that's just the natural conflict. This "problem" has now been magnified several fold. I call it the "great depression" because when you're trying to sell something to these people that's going to solve one or more very big problems for them, the prospect's internal "political" problems between these two Departments can become so acute that they can literally freeze everything for months on end. They can put a complete halt on progress. This is against the interests of their own organization. Yet, based on our inheritance from the twentieth century, it is perhaps inevitable. Allow me to explain!

The twenty-first century is an exciting time for us software folk. The latter part of the twentieth century has left a residue of hugely inefficient server farms and massive, inefficiently deployed computing power, serving very large scale consumer and business communities who continue to increasingly adopt the internet as their preferred "channel" of contact with their service providers. The whole I.T. boom, hype, explosion,

burst – whatever you like to call it, accelerated the
discovery of new business models like Application
Service Provision, extranet application deployment, new
"multi-channel" service delivery possibilities and a host
of other, new software technologies in the middleware
and transaction processing environments. The key word
in all of this is "discovery". We *discovered*. At the time
we discovered, we didn't have a lot of experience with
these new delivery mechanisms or technologies –
because we hadn't discovered them until now! So what
did we do? When we realized how good they were, we
developed new software applications, designed new
levels of reusability, security, performance improvement
and integrity into our systems. But, and here's the issue,
because we were early in our discovery phase, we
hadn't necessarily thought through the full implications
for these new systems based on massive increases in
demand, the increasing need to automate new, more
complex processes on top of this new "infrastructure", or
how the demand for these new systems would deliver
competitive advantage – or competitive disadvantage.

The bottom line? We arrived in the twenty first century
with these massive, inefficient server farms being
managed, maintained and evolved (in so far as they can
be) by truck-loads of I.T. personnel. They are housed in
"mega" concrete bunkers, have as much continuity of

business backup infrastructure as was possible and cost a fortune to run just on utilities alone!

So how is the conflict magnified? The business team's focus is cost efficiency. We've a bit more experience with the new technologies and delivery models now. The server farms can be radically compacted, performance can be massively improved, security can now be bullet proofed, continuity of business can now be almost instantaneous if you're prepared to pay for it and software solutions can now extend across the entire organization without being tied to departmental "silos". I.T. personnel themselves have now entered the targeting range of replacement automation – and they don't like it! What makes matters even worse is that they must necessarily play a part in their own demise!

Can you see any big ticket savings here for your big fish before they even get to the application efficiencies? Welcome to the next development phase in our industry!

Disqualification from a MSA

There are occasions when you may not make it through the due diligence process. Whatever the reason, your prospect is faced with an often tough decision – to either end its dialogue with you or to find a way it can still work with you. The good news is that all is not lost if you don't make it to a Master Services Agreement. It can however get a bit messy, but if your prospect is determined enough to get your product or service, it has some options open to it. To keep my focus on MSA's, all I will do is list them here to give you some ideas of what you can shoot for.

1. The prospect can secure your company and service provision by taking equity in your business. Clearly a wider process is involved here. Before engaging it, you obviously will consider what influence this would have on your future growth, your competitive position in your wider market, whether it makes investment sense and so on.

2. You can plug-in to another preferred supplier's MSA. It is not at all unknown for a prospect to come to a fee-based arrangement with another of its preferred vendors to act as a non-executive facilitator of your engagement. These are perfectly legitimate and legal (of course!) business arrangements, but prospects tend not to like them. They require several warranties and indemnities to completely eliminate any risk to the enabling vendor. They go against the very core of the reason why a MSA exists in the first place; to procure the project from a vendor that

is safe and compliant. When a "plug-in" engagement goes wrong, there's a major clean-up operation required.

3. You can still continue your engagement on the basis of a more basic purchase agreement, but these are usually significantly constrained in both budget and the nature of work that can be procured. Also, for each new piece of work to be placed on you, the process must be repeated. Prospects don't like this either!

4. You can partner with another major player to jointly bid your solution. This is very acceptable to bigger prospects. However, they will be watching closely the margin that your bigger partner is taking on your software and services. They don't want to "pay double" as they see it. On the flip-side of this, if your partner cannot sustain their margin on the front-end with the potential client, they'll squeeze you on the back-end. So think twice before you take this route, but it may be a good option for you.

I firmly believe that if you've done a good job of selling yourself, your team, your company and your solution, and the prospect genuinely wants to work with you, the prospect will find a path that takes you all the way to a MSA.

Before finally accepting that a MSA is not available to you, be sure to fully explore every possible corrective and corroborative action that could put it back on track. People with whom you have a good working and personal relationship tend to go far out of their way to help you. Persevere.

CHAPTER 5

Intellectual Property and Know-How

When you actually attain big ticket value recognition for your intellectual property and know-how in the marketplace, you automatically become a tasty morsel for some very big and potentially nasty fish on both sides of the buy / sell divide! Although this is exactly where you want to be from a market value and net worth perspective, it is not to say that it is always pleasant! Even before you get to the finishing line, there may be some very big hurdles to cross that were not of your own or your prospect's creation – at least not intentionally! These hurdles often come in the form of Great White Sharks!

Big Buyers and Great White Sharks!

Once you decide to compete on the big scale, you are entering a market where there are typically big competitors – often predatory ones. Big to massive ticket projects are the preserve of very big fish on the supply side also. Their predatory instinct is to quickly consume any small fish that dare to put their big ticket deal in any jeopardy whatsoever. It is not at all unknown, indeed it is usual, where one of these big vendor fish is involved that they will go to major lengths to be retained by the big buyer fish to "validate" your solution – i.e. you've got to get past them first. For the buyer, to have one of these big fish validate your solution, is to take significant risk out of the process, since they would have the seal of approval from a major external party.

Not all big vendor fish are sharks. Indeed some are whales and are happy for you to swim in their wake. But when you encounter a great white shark, you have strayed into deep waters indeed, because more often than not, your deal is floundering before it has even commenced!

There are two reasons why these sharks may be interested in you.

1) You have intellectual content that could leverage more of their services, hardware or system software based added value to the customer.

2) You have gotten in the way of a major deal that they were about to conclude either directly or with another software vendor.

So let's look at them.

Leverage

It is quite possible that the services they want to provide your prospect with, on the back of your intellectual property, are the very same services that you were hoping to negotiate directly. Now you are in a position that you are being asked by your prospect to collaborate with this third party shark in order to validate your solution.

You can do a couple of things here:

> **Refuse**. By doing this, you run the risk of exclusion, since you are preventing your prospect from significantly reducing its perceived risk in the project. Of course, you may have a unique solution and the prospect may have to live with your refusal. But for convenience here, let's assume your prospect has an alternative.
>
> You may refuse on the basis that the release of intellectual know-how from you to the shark would jeopardize your wider competitive position in the marketplace. Whilst you may be working with this particular shark on this project, you may be competing with it on the next.
>
> **Conditionally agree** – but assert your position. Agree to collaborate with the shark based on these provisions:

- That the shark not only signs a direct non-disclosure and non-compete agreement (NDA / NCA) with you, but that it formally becomes a party to the prospect's NDA. In other words, the prospect is accepting liability for any breach from the shark.

- That the shark is explicitly precluded from any services relating to the project that your organization is capable of providing directly! This of course is the chunk of flesh which you have prised off with your little piranha teeth! You can, if you wish, further add that, in cases where you are unable to provide the services directly, that you are given a finite period of time within which to put in place whatever resources were required should you so wish.

Asserting your position like this in the presence of a shark is the very best way you can maintain credibility with your prospect and keep control of the project. You are playing for big stakes here and knowing the nature of the fish in the vicinity will help you a great deal not just in landing your big fish, but doing it in the right way. Do it again and again and it becomes systematic, you get good at it and you can repeat it more easily.

You're In The Way

In this case, a great white shark will want to either get rid of you or work with, but dominate you. To get rid of you, it may try to either undermine your solution in some way to the prospect or put itself between you and the prospect in such a way that you cannot regain a position of control in the project. If it is unable to get rid of you, it will want to work with you, but in a way that leaves you very much subservient to them in the project. Should this happen, you will have lost your vantage point in the project – more on that later. You will be moving from big-to-mega ticket to medium-to-big ticket.

Your very best protection from this kind of predatory activity is to continue to nurture and maintain your senior executive relationships. It is at the senior executive level that the shark will attempt to inflict most damage on you. Bear in mind also that these sharks are extremely well educated and trained in the art of senior executive relations. You have no choice but to become every bit as good as or better than them in nurturing these relationships. If you are at the point that senior executives discuss strategy and competitive position with you, that's a good sign! The best way to get good at this is to do it regularly and continuously. If you are working at a distance, remember that out of sight is indeed out of mind and you will need to manage your time accordingly.

If the shark discovers that you are, for the moment untouchable, and it may persevere with several new attempts to undermine you before it does, it may appear to take you seriously. It may even reach a point that it declares you as a "player" and that it is better off working with you than working against you. Of course, it is unlikely, unless it is leading to something else, to be comfortable acting in a subcontract capacity.

You should continue to always be inquisitive as to the shark's added value in the project. Never believe for a moment that it has accepted your position as a "player". It is just when you believe the shark has moved on to new waters that it may make a deadly strike!

Thus far, you may have sensed a note of cynicism when it comes to sharks and small to medium sized software companies. I have experienced friendly sharks too. But what I am advising is that you are safer to approach these fish with very great caution indeed until you are absolutely satisfied of their intentions.

The Partnering Decision

A significant consequence of concluding your first two or three mega-ticket projects is a wider market belief that you have created something of real value. You will likely attract new contacts from the vendor, buyer and financial communities as well as your own software industry. The value of these contacts is of course, what you do with them. One valuable route you can take is to directly leverage your intellectual property. You can do this by putting in place teaming agreements with some of the big vendor fish to pursue new specific opportunities, or to build full partnership agreements to target the wider market.

Whatever you do, you have a decision to make. Is it your desire to continue to target combined software and services projects or is your preference to focus specifically on developing intellectual property and let others provide the services?

This is a big decision. Whatever you decide, it is my own belief that software company that does not maintain its direct hands-on experience of customer implementation, is destined to fall down the ladder of domain knowledge. Many companies have lived and died to regret passing over their services business to third party resellers and integrators. Others of course have flourished.

However, it is not necessary to maintain this exposure across the board. For example, it is not unreasonable to maintain direct customer services in one market and be a supplier of software only in another. If you believe that you can build your organization to be capable to servicing customers directly irrespective of geography, then you may have viable alternatives both ways. There are also middle ground options where you can consider joint venture service companies to form a "practice" around implementing and tailoring your solution.

Risks of Intellectual Property Leakage

If you read Andy Grove's book "*Only the Paranoid Survive*", you might be tempted to build a fortress around the capability you have developed and forever remain small! The reality is that, with even moderate precautions, the evolution and further development of your own company's domain knowledge and intellectual know-how should out-pace any organization's attempt to benefit from the pieces you left behind. "Moderate precautions" may include:

- good non-disclosure and confidentiality agreements
- good licensing strategies and agreements
- avoid walk-through demonstrations making their way into the public domain
- avoid customer's user documentation being put up on a non-secured area of the internet for download by end-users

- avoid unnecessarily detailed sales or marketing materials

- controlled release of source code and conditions on its use

- employment contracts that prevent key personnel from joining competitive organizations for at least twelve months after they leave your employment

- effective internal control of electronic and printed documentation such as business use case definitions, specifications, models etc...

- Last but perhaps not least, avoid being obliged to work with third parties who require access to your know-how or code to deliver their parts of the project!

A final word of caution is appropriate on protecting your intellectual property. In the modern world, the software industry has become a truly global marketplace with internationalized knowledge-based industries flourishing in every part of the planet. Unfortunately, not all countries have yet put in place the legislation which properly protects international software copyright. Once your documentation or code makes its way into these countries you can expect flagrant disregard for copyright in the form of competitive solutions, unauthorized licensing and public access to documentation, making it available

to all your competition irrespective of geography
over the internet if they find out about it!

Nevertheless, fear of others acquiring parts of your
know-how or having controlled access to your
intellectual content is not a good reason for standing
still.

CHAPTER 6

Negotiating a Master Software Licensing and Services Agreement

This chapter covers a number of specific negotiating positions you can adopt during various stages of the actual Master Services Agreement negotiation. It will also give you some powerful tactics that will help you to support your position throughout. Consider it as an "MSA negotiation walkthrough" that will get you well up the experience ladder before your negotiation even commences.

Bear in mind that it is not my intention here to tutor you in general negotiating skills. The chapter will give you a heads-up on many issues which, by pre-empting them, will give you more "think time" to strategize your position on each. At the end of it, you can reasonably expect that your ability to negotiate MSAs will have improved, that you can deliver more favourable outcomes for your company and that the monetary value of your MSAs will increase - significantly.

Introduction

You already know that the "negotiating stage" is not a point in time that you "arrive" at. It has been going on since the beginning of your contact with the prospect. However, there *will* come a point in time, probably when the prospect's purchasing team engages, that you will be called upon to negotiate the actual content of the

Master Services Agreement. That's what this chapter is about.

Getting to here is great. You've passed your due diligence on all fronts and have come up to the mark as an organization that your prospect would like to do business with. But there are no prizes for second place - and you are not home and dried! Put the champagne on ice for now and play it hopefully but cautiously in the boardroom. There may also be another vendor in the wings.

The prospect can play you a few ways. They may declare the existence of the second potential vendor to keep you honest. It is not unknown that, in fact there may not be a second vendor. Because this is a complex negotiation and you are close to several different individuals on the prospect side, there is a good chance that you would find this out. Because of this, it is unusual for this tactic to be used as the ploy is too obvious.

They may decide not to declare the second vendor – but of course, you may already know that there is one, or even who it is! Where a second vendor exists and your prospect fully engages you in the negotiation, it is clearly a good sign. It usually means that, should they fail to reach an agreement with you, the second prospect will be engaged.

A prospect may *parallel run* two separate negotiations when the stakes are high, when there is not a major distance between the two vendors – even if one is preferred, or if there is an expectation that the negotiation is going to be "bloody"! "Bloody" means that there is an aggressive agenda about to be played by the prospect. It could literally mean millions of dollars straight off your bottom line.

Irrespective of what your prospect's motive is in declaring or otherwise a second vendor, you should conduct your negotiation without consideration of other parties. Outside of the main negotiating "strand", the other interacting "strands" with the Business team, I.T. team etc... will continue. You should prime your team to keep their ears open for any hints of competitive involvement throughout their interactions. Sometimes, a heads-up here can help you through a difficult stage in your negotiation.

A Few Basic Pre-Negotiation Pitfalls

Before you ever reach the MSA negotiating stage, there will be several opportunities for you to grossly undermine your own eventual negotiating position! I will list a few of the common ones.

Don't Negotiate Prematurely

Every now and then from your first contact with your prospect to final signature, people will try to score "internal brownie points" by getting some kind of concession from you. This "scoring" is not always choreographed on the prospect side, but nevertheless satisfies some people's need to go running to their boss and say "I've got these guys to agree to ..."! These things do however tend to get recorded and brought up just at a time when you wished you hadn't conceded.

A strange thing about this *scoring* business is that the scorer doesn't have to be a part of the organizational function responsible for that *type* of score! For example, someone in your prospect's I.T. team could tell you confidentially that your competitor has come in at seventy percent of your price on the standard daily rate and that there's no way that they will agree to pay more than that. After lots of discussion, you agree to match the price if that's going to make the difference. What you would not have realized was that your actual negotiation had not yet started, that you did not need to make a decision there and then and that the individual was not authorized to make that negotiating play with you. You would be better off by replying "That's good to know – thanks!" – and pigeon-holing it for later consideration. If pushed, a good position to take is to state your willingness to look at it, but in the *context* of other related matters which would also need to be considered.

Other, even big-scale premature negotiations also happen. A very real example is where your "Champion" offers to confidentially proof-read your proposal's executive summary before you officially submit your proposal. He or she discovers that your license fee is listed at twenty cents per transaction and advises you that the internal transaction fee target was eighteen cents. Do you concede there and then or do you probe to see if you left it at twenty cents, would it exclude you from the short list? It won't. You're close enough for them to believe that they will get you down during the real negotiation. In fact, it is highly desirable to have your financial proposal pitched at about 30% above what you think your prospect is comfortable with.

A word of caution is appropriate here. It may indeed be necessary for you to make certain concessions to get to the negotiating table. Be careful therefore to assess the distinction between a concession you don't need to make at this stage and one you do. In the cases where you do need to concede, it will be obvious. The heads-up on it is unlikely to come from one individual – it will usually be a friendly grouping that advises you. The issue will usually be quite dramatic in its nature. For example, instead of being 20% out on a fee, you were 100% out, or instead of only offering to host it directly, you agree to deploy it to the prospect's data centre.

You Have No Shortage of Resources

Some people make the mistake of using the resource issue as a time pressure on the prospect to make a decision. They become exasperated with the length of time it is taking to get to the beginning of the negotiation. It goes something like this – "Unless you can complete the agreement within the coming sixty days, we have no choice but to assign the team to other projects." Apart from being usually an obvious ploy, it divulges, correctly or incorrectly, that you have limited resources. Even if they could complete the agreement within sixty days, they now believe that you can only carry out so much work on the project due to limited resources. You will have significantly undermined your ability during the negotiation to up the ante on your share of development and additional services work.

Whilst you should never claim limited resources, it is more than reasonable, indeed advisable for you to claim *valuable* resources. This goes something like "We really need to put our engagement on a commercial footing as it is locking up many of my best people with no guarantee of a successful outcome". This is something that your prospect will empathize with more and sets the stage for you to negotiate a temporary fund to cover your costs until the contract can be signed.

Get the Big Picture before Negotiating the Little Ones

As your pre-sale engagement progresses, and as you now know, you will regularly encounter instances when certain concessions were suggested to you – usually politely! You also know that in most cases, rather than concede, you note them for later action. What you are doing is making a record of some of the issues you have been made aware of, which have been stated as being of value to the prospect. The negotiation itself is where you will discover the extent of that value and what you may be able to gain in exchange.

However, what you are also doing is not agreeing to anything until you get a big picture view of what the complete negotiating landscape looks like. A great way to get this at the beginning of the negotiation stage is through the use of a *term sheet* which is covered later.

Being on the buyer side of a negotiation, your prospect will go to work on you point by point, sub-clause by sub-clause, one issue at a time. It is true to say that, generally, a Master Services Agreement is structured in a way that succumbs quite easily to a sequential negotiation. But this is not always the case. There are often linkages between certain parts of the MSA which can be negotiated together or concessions exchanged. Your term sheet will help you identify and relate these parts together.

Mind Your Existing Business

Given the period of time that an MSA negotiation can take, a critical pitfall to avoid is the assumption that you are near the finishing line! Avoid the temptation to think that the impact on your current business will be short-lived. There is no easy formula for cloning your people just yet! Be certain to continue to discharge your responsibility to the rest of the business and keep one foot outside of the negotiation.

The pre-contract resource draw on your team is often very significant. Your team may have to retrospectively "clean up" documentation for their software in preparation for detailed scrutiny. They may have to review or create new reams of documentation relating to processes, methods or procedures. They may have to re-create new disaster recovery processes.

Quite apart from what they *may* have to do, they *will* need to fully engage the prospect's business and technical teams, build relationships, respond to emails, fill forms and do whatever can be reasonably expected by the prospect. All this without any guarantee of reward at the end!

Reassigning a significant percentage of your team's time in this way needs a counter plan to ensure your business can continue as normal.

The Term Sheet

Since it is not unusual to be at some geographical distance from your prospect, it is normal practice that much of your negotiation exchanges will take place by telephone. A "current" term sheet makes this process practical.

A term sheet is a spreadsheet which is built by either party, usually the buyer and is updated and emailed after each negotiating session. It is a record of each milestone between your present point in time and final signature of the agreement. Note that it is not just the negotiation issues it records; it also records the specific milestones to be complied with. For example, your prospect may require your hosting site to pass its security audit. This will be recorded on the term sheet as it is a condition of the Master Services Agreement.

Any change to either party's position in any aspect of the term sheet is recorded and an update emailed. It also helps to maintain a big picture focus on the agreement as a whole by maintaining visibility on its entirety.

A good term sheet will have the following columns listed at the top of your worksheet from left to right:

Draft Master Services Agreement paragraph number

If a draft agreement exists (it usually does), this is the sequential occurrence of each issue as it appears in the draft agreement – *not* a prioritized list; it is of course not a good idea for *any* side to reveal what its priorities actually are!

Issue title / heading
You should use the draft agreement wording so that you can confirm the numeric reference in the previous column.

Issue description

This is the buyer's "layman's description" of the MSA paragraph. It can include reasons or rationale behind the paragraph and a clear statement of what is expected from the vendor.

Vendor position on the issue

Entered by you, this is your comment on why the said paragraph is not acceptable to you as it stands.

Buyer position on the issue

Your prospect will document their view on the issue here. This is not the same as any reasons that may be given in the issue description. The difference is that while "issue description" may outline standard policy, the "buyer position" may suggest that standard policy may not be enforceable in this instance or that they would be flexible on the issue. Of course, it may also state that their current position is that this cannot change.

Potential middle ground alternatives

Entries are typically made in this column by both parties. It records on-going *ideas*, as they happen, that might lead to agreement on the particular issue.

Current status

It is useful to colour-code here: blue=resolved, red=open.

While the term sheet can run to several pages (adjust your page settings to fit one page wide), it is truly a major help in easing the administration of negotiations which take place over a period of months. They also allow you to instantly report internally on the status of the opportunity and to easily recall what all of the outstanding issues and milestones are.

Into the Agreement

Now that you've exchanged the opening salvos in the negotiation, let's now look at the areas of the Master Services Agreement where you may be expected to negotiate.

Warranties, Indemnities & Refunds!

The agreement will oblige you to make several indemnities and warranties which are reasonable and with which you should have no problem. However, there will be a few where you may have a problem! Specifically, these may include (a) compliance with specifications, and (b) refunds!

Compliance with Specifications

A simple trap to fall into here, especially where customization and bespoke work is involved, is that your prospect may require you to comply with its "specifications". On the face of it, this seems reasonable, but what constitutes its "specifications"? They often mean a high level requirements definition which is not only open to interpretation but puts control of the warranty firmly in your prospect's court.

> You should instead ensure that the required warranty is phrased clearly enough that it refers to compliance with *your own* published specifications. In the case of bespoke software, you should be the one to produce the specifications. Whilst there will be elements of the requirement which you will know with confidence that you will meet or exceed, there may be others such as performance or even certain functionality, that will require testing, benchmarking or experimentation before you should commit to producing its specification.

Refunds

In the negotiation, you will be fighting hard for as much payment up front as possible and as much medium and longer term recurring income as is feasible to agree. You may also be trading these off against each other.

The last place you want to find yourself is in a position of having to refund a license fee. Not only does this hurt at the time of refund, but as long as the risk of a refund exists, i.e. that there is a deliverable to be made before the refund issue is off the table, you are unlikely to be able to recognize the income from an accounting perspective. Your Chief Financial Officer will love you if can safeguard revenue recognition on the deal!

Your prospect may want a refund situation to arise where you fail to meet specifications (emphasizing point (a) above) or where your software unintentionally had an impact on another part of their environment.

Counter the refund idea on the basis that your prospect is primarily responsible for pre-rollout testing and more so, acceptance. Even though they will be collaborating with you, and whilst you expect that no major issue will escape your combined rigorous testing methods, it is not reasonable that you could be held accountable for your prospect's acceptance testing. It is also not reasonable that you be held accountable for an issue arising that neither you nor the prospect could have anticipated until the solution went live. This is the prospect's risk in the project, not yours! Rather than negotiate its risk out, your prospect needs to work with you

towards building test and validation methods that
design it out!

Statements of Work

Statements of Work (SoW) are attachments to the
Master Services Agreement. There will be multiple
statements of work, drawn up and attached as needed,
each one relating to a specific piece of the project. They
contain details of the exact work to be done, when it is
to be delivered and work-specific payment conditions
beyond the umbrella payment terms in the main MSA.

A key consideration over the deals ahead of you is an
awareness of, and management of, the timing and
sequence of your statements of work. What this means
is that since SoW's define what and when you get paid
for, managing the smooth transition from one to the
other keeps the project flowing and income generated!

Each individual SoW must be singularly constructed with
deliverables and timing, by and from both parties set in
stone. In themselves, they are complex documents and
take time to build and agree. The danger continually
exists that a project will be "frozen" between the
completion of one part of the project and the
commencement of another if the next SoW is not ready
at the time the previous one is complete. Commencing

the SoW building and negotiating process must therefore precede the completion of the current SoW, often by several months. The first SoW will usually be negotiated during the closing stages of the main Master Services Agreement.

It is also not unusual that more than one SoW can be current at a particular time, with separate as well as overlapping teams involved. Resource permitting, this is the ideal situation.

The need to have multiple SoW's *in play,* at varying stages of construction enforces visibility on the project as a whole as well as maintaining delivery momentum.

Competitive Advantage

In a big ticket project, especially one that will be driven by a Master Services Agreement, the issue of competitive advantage is usually fairly high on your prospect's agenda. Despite this, there are degrees to which different prospects want to push it. At its extreme, and if an opportunity exists, your prospect may want to reach an exclusive deal with you. Generally, exclusive contracts are not advisable. Because they are increasingly seen as anti-competitive, legislation in many countries across the globe are making it difficult to support a challenge when they are breached. Despite this, some organizations will still pursue it. I suggest a particular angle you might play on the exclusivity issue in the "Ten Hot Tips" chapter.

Other ways your prospect may wish to deal with the competitive advantage issue are:

Most Favoured Customer

In the MSA, you may be asked to commit to one or two elements in a "most favoured customer" context. Specifically, you may even be asked not to engage another competitor on a similar project for at least a six month period. This is effectively a six month exclusivity period. This is often the case where your competitor is part of an oligopoly; they have only a relatively small number of competitors, each with moderate market share. This is an interesting request not least because it is suggesting a six month period. From when? Now? The point of contract signature? Does that mean, in fact twelve months? Will they pay for that? Or will they sign tomorrow? Get the picture? So probe it and get some value for it, if of course it suits you at all to concede it!

The other part of "most preferred customer" is a warrant from you that you will not license or service another of its competitors for a price less than your prospect's final contract price. Whilst this is generally reasonable, you may not be all that comfortable with it when you consider that your current prospect might only be half the size of its competitors and that you feel you should be free to strike volume-based agreements with the others. You may be able to negotiate parity or better based on volume or transactions, registered users etc...

You may even decide that you are unlikely to be able to engage your prospect's competitors within a six month period, let alone give them price parity. In this case, and as you know this issue is quite high on the agenda, you can leverage it to put an extra expediency on conclusion of the contract. You may for example, agree six months from today's date, or agree to maintain your prospect at best price for a period of time from today's date.

Intellectual know-how and innovative ideas

Where proprietary, bespoke parts of the overall solution are to be specified and / or developed by you, your prospect will want to prevent you from using it in any competitive solution. There are a few considerations here. The bespoke solution may indeed hold some innovative idea that directly delivers differentiation in the marketplace or a significant cost advantage to your prospect. Professionally as well as ethically, you must preserve the integrity of this advantage. Nevertheless, the reality is that while your prospect may retain the intellectual property ownership on this software, the intellectual *know-how* cannot be removed from your employee's minds. Yet! Your prospect knows this and may well reserve these parts of the project for its own internal team. However, assuming it will be you that does the work, it places a certain pressure on the prospect (and this will not be forgotten as the project progresses) to keep your team members who worked on a sensitive aspect of the project, engaged in other parts of the project sensitive or otherwise – usually well after the initial work! So you should strive to get involved in the sensitive aspects of the project as they contribute to your on-going value to your customer.

License: Nature and Authorities

A previous chapter discussed various licensing permutations you can use in a MSA. As a general rule, you should (and will need to) go to some lengths to describe the actual authorities conferred by the license being issued. Your prospect will want the license to cover every conceivable future context in which they might want to use it. This may seem reasonable, and indeed, as long as the envisioned usage remains reasonable, you do not need to make it unnecessarily complex. Things to be generally avoided would include such rights as sub-licensing and distribution unless they are a specific part of the overall agreement.

However, what might represent a reasonable "usage context" for your prospect, may not always be reasonable in your view. For example,

Third party service provision

In particular when your prospect will build its own complete commercial, technical and support competency around your solution and when the solution will be housed in the prospect's Data Centre, your prospect may envision a situation that it may provide application services based on your solution to other, external, usually smaller players in the industry. It may attempt to negotiate the rights to do so as part of this MSA.

Assuming this is not something you want to allow, you might counter this on the basis that (1) it would compete directly with you or another of your partners in the wider market who would pay you substantially for the privilege of doing it, and (2) it would provide a service to parties who have not purchased a license from you.

Of course, this could be an interesting opportunity for you to incrementally license your prospect as a third party application service provider with appropriate reimbursement to you. You may find that, unless the prospect has a currently visible intention to do this, they will put it to one side. Do not let it get lost however, as it could provide an additional future revenue source for you after the project is rolled out.

Future Affiliates

Your prospect is likely to request the license to cover all of its existing and future "affiliates". It may define an affiliate as a body where 51% of the stock is held by your prospect. Generally there is no issue here. When it comes to future affiliates however, some important issues can arise. In particular, the area of mergers and acquisitions holds some pitfalls which you should try to avoid. Your prospect will want to allow for license transfer to the newly acquired or merged entity. Be careful here because this can often be embedded into a clause where it is easy to overlook or be read casually in a paragraph that seems otherwise OK. I deal with this issue in the next chapter.

Intellectual Property

There are two basic contexts in which the issue of intellectual property may arise in a MSA;

Acquired ownership in your software

This is where the prospect purchases your software outright, including an ownership interest in your source code. In this instance, your prospect has the right to do with it whatever it wishes, potentially including redistribution, sub-licensing, provision of application services and modifying the code as it deems fit. Of course, once the code is modified, even slightly, by a third party, you cannot support it. Potentially significant revenue is immediately lost to you once you agree to such an ownership right.

The good news is that, unless the deal is of an outright purchase nature, big organizations don't like taking something that is complex and modifying it in any way. They usually buy the supplier instead!

Ownership of IP on bespoke developments

In general, you should try to negotiate the IP rights to anything you develop. It can be useful to link back to this issue when you are negotiating your rate sheet (such matters are usually left until the end). No matter what rates you have proposed, your prospect will negotiate you down. Retention of intellectual property on anything developed on the project is a good value exchange as you can correctly claim that you get a fair opportunity to recover any lost income you may concede on the rate sheet. Areas with real and pre-specified competitive advantage could reasonably be *agreed* in advance to be excluded.

Your Rate Sheet

Your team will be involved in the project at various levels of responsibility. If you wished, you could negotiate a flat rate with your prospect. However, you may be better off by proposing a rate sheet with different rates based on project function or role. You will need to be careful here to avoid your best or more expensive people being asked to fill certain project roles that are not sufficiently senior or influential. This can arise when your prospect insists on assigning their own personnel to a particular role, yet wants specific individuals from your team to participate in the group. In this case, you might consider negotiating your rate sheet based on individual seniority within your own company.

For the reasons discussed under *Competitive Advantage*, your prospect will most likely be keen to absorb as many of your best people as possible into the project. If you can afford to assign these particular individuals to the project full time, you will obviously benefit from the higher rates quoted for these people.

No matter what rates you propose, there is a good probability that they will be negotiated. If you are a small or medium sized business, it is sometimes frustrating when you know that the prospect is already paying one of the "big" external consulting practices or systems integrators, $3,000 - $5,000 per day for knowledge and advice that your company would be significantly more capable of providing in such a specialist domain. Despite this, your big fish may only be prepared to offer you $800 per day on the basis of rates that were quoted by other parties or resource that could be locally sourced. These are clearly two extremes so the final resting point of your rate sheet will lie somewhere in between.

You will also discover that, frequently, the involvement of one the big consultancies are part of an on-going Master Services Agreement that they already have in place. It is interesting to note that, despite not being the most knowledgeable or experienced in this particular area, they are still retained under the MSA.

These are basically bulk services purchasing contracts where a major block of "days" are committed over a period of time. The fact that your prospect may be obligated under one can have a major influence on bid outcomes. In particular, it can make it dangerous to compete on the basis of your rate sheet (you wouldn't, would you?).

As far as your prospect is concerned, whether they like it or not, they may be obliged to use these services even though they know that you would do it better. The effect of this is that because your prospect has to pay for the services irrespective if whether it uses you or not, it tends to neutralize any initiative you may take relating to your rate sheet. So before you do, be sure that another MSA does not exist that impacts the project.

Fixed Bidding

In many cases, you will be asked at RFP stage to *fix bid* all or parts of the project. Fixed bidding is when you agree to fully deliver on a part of the work for less than a maximum cost. If the actual costs to deliver it exceed your maximum bid price, then you must incur the difference. Should you come in under budget, you may still get paid the full fixed bid price; you are compensated for the risk you took. In other cases, your deal may be structured such that, where you come in under budget, the prospect benefits. The former however is more popular.

When you are confident (minimal risk), fixed bidding has its advantages.

- You may effectively have a guaranteed upside.

- Payments can be easier to administer

- Income can be more accurately forecasted

- For your prospect, perceived risk is reduced and payments are straightforward.

The major risk in fixed bidding is obvious – failure to deliver on time can be very costly. A less obvious risk, yet one that needs a major heads-up is *control* of deliverables. When a "Statement of Work" is fixed bid, whether for customization of part of the software solution or for a piece of bespoke software to be integrated with the wider solution, the commitment is typically to complete the work within a defined timescale. Unfortunately, the sub-deliverables within the overall statement of work are not always under your control. It may be the case that you are waiting for your prospect to respond with something that you need before you can progress the work. Sometimes this can take quite a while!

You need therefore to build a clause into your MSA which caters for this. You need to pre-empt what the exact prospect deliverable will be and to oblige the prospect to responding within a set timeframe. Failure to do so will extend the delivery timescale.

OK, you can legislate for this, but here's where the real problem lies – say you're waiting three months for one of the project teams to send you a requirements definition for a part of the project. At the beginning of that three month period, you are not able to predict that it is going to take three months. So what do you do? Wait? Have some of your best people twiddling their thumbs while you are waiting? Remember that the prospect has a fixed bid from you so it costs them no more money – time at worst. Despite their best intentions, they simply may not be able to get an earlier reply to you. In the meantime, you are unable to assign your people to another project because you don't know how long they will be available for!

This is somewhat more difficult to legislate for. An idea that has worked in the past – but has to be negotiated, is to build in a notice period of, say thirty days, for re-engagement in the project if the prospect misses a deadline by more than say, fourteen days. Your prospect may not appreciate this as they will expect you to immediately pick up from where you left off when they deliver whatever it is you were waiting for! But if you think about it, your argument here is very sustainable and can directly result in lost revenue for you by not being able to engage your team in other work. Placing such a pressure to deliver on the prospect's team is actually healthy in an overall project context.

The bottom line is – don't fixed bid unless you are one hundred percent confident of your delivery and that your prospect agrees to the above or similar conditions.

Termination

Lots of sensitivities exist around the whole area of termination. Despite popular opinion, the circumstances which lead to termination are not always a fault by either party! If the agreement permits it, your prospect may be able to terminate your MSA without even giving you a reason – and this can be dear to some people's hearts!

Two things are important relating to termination; the reason or basis for it and the obligations of the respective parties. Here are a few contexts.

No cause / Convenience

Termination for no cause allows your prospect to end the agreement without giving you a reason. One reason why a prospect might wish to include this clause is where they acquired or merged with another company who had their own perhaps proprietary solution which could replace yours at a lower cost or provide another advantage.

Your prospect would like to have no obligation to you whatsoever in this circumstance. Believe it or not, your prospect may even attempt to negotiate a refund from you as it will no longer use or get value from your solution!

Where a "no cause" termination is required, you should consider negotiating a prospect obligation to pay in full any outstanding license amounts – including all amounts not called down, payment up the maximum of committed professional services which your contract may have included and payment for full team engagement for a notice period duration – say three months.

You may even consider negotiating an additional financial amount as compensation for loss of income since you will have committed a significant team and resource to the project based on its entirety.

Never agree to a refund and never accept a no cause termination without full discharge of the entire MSA amount.

Breach by you

You may breach the agreement either by design or by accident. By breaching by design, you may be acting unethically and should bear in mind that your honour and reputation could be at stake. There is no circumstance that a breach by you, just to escape the contract, is acceptable. Once you enter into it, you must complete it.

Despite this, conscious supplier breaches of contract have been known to occur. Upon analysis, such breaches tend to be for reasons of greed (a bigger opportunity arose with a competitor) or fear (a fixed bid contract could not be delivered on). Your customer will clearly want to have a major hold over you if you breach by design. Included within this could be many pre-litigation conditions including the retention of full ownership rights to the software and a maximum financial penalty.

You may breach by accident if say, you licensed the software to another organization that you did not consider competitive, but were prohibited from doing so in the agreement as long as your prospect considered them competitive.

In an accidental breach situation, the MSA should include remedies whereby you are given the opportunity of resolving the breach within a reasonable time. Failure to do so would be considered a purposeful breach. I have never encountered a situation where accidental breach could not be resolved either through discussion with the customer or through the remedies in the MSA.

Breach by your Customer

Your prospect may also breach by accident or design. Accidental breach might have occurred through an unauthorized use of the license, say by an unlisted affiliate. Accidental breaches by the customer should also be allowed time to be resolved using the MSA's remedies.

A customer's breach by design might have occurred because a reason arose which made it no longer in the interests of your customer to be committed to you. Such reasons might include your engagement with a competitor even though this was not precluded in the MSA, a change in the direction of your company, or indeed, a change in the direction of your customer!

In the event of a customer breach, where fault clearly lies with your customer, you should ensure that the customer is obliged to pay in full any outstanding license amounts – including all amounts not called down, payment of the full outstanding, committed professional services which your contract may have included, payment in lieu of your agreed notice period plus a fixed premature termination amount which your prospect must pay to compensate you for loss of income. This latter payment is clearly easier to negotiate here than in the event of a no-cause termination.

For performance and other reasons

There may be instances when one or other party is deemed to have breached the agreement, but where no easily identified fault lies. In the worst case, the parties "blame" each other. For this reason, it is highly recommended that both you and your prospect make every effort to pre-empt as many potential issues as you can, that could cause such a situation to arise, and deal with them in the agreement. By covering them in the agreement, you are dealing with the issue of "doubt" by clearly defining who is responsible for what.

For example, several MSA's in the past have run into issues associated with performance of the live production system. This can mean end user response times, lapses in security, information delivery etc... If you have negotiated objectively, the performance issue should not be one that you hold exclusively unless you can be certain that you can replicate exactly your customer's live production environment. Instead, especially where the live solution will be rolled out on an internet delivery model, the performance issue is something that you jointly hold and collaborate on to resolve. Where scalability cannot be tested in advance beyond laboratory based recursive testing, performance in a live environment should be a shared risk.

Your Financial Proposal and Payment Terms

Your financial proposal must travel the great distance between what was presented in your RFP response and what was finally signed in the MSA. There is actually a good chance that one bears little resemblance to the other! Even its fundamental structure can change. For example, what started out as a transaction fee based proposal might have ended up as an outright license purchase. Or what started out as a perpetual development license may have ended up as an annually licensed or leased service.

Irrespective of the finally agreed model, it is likely to include the following embedded or explicit components:

- Core software license; perpetual, annual or transaction fee.

- Customization work; development work requiring an intimate knowledge of your existing software.

- Bespoke work; development work requiring a less intimate knowledge of your software.

- Maintenance and Support services; usually an annually recurring percentage of your license fee or based on full time equivalent personnel.

- Project and executive management services

Your prospect's mission in negotiating your financial proposal will be to link any and all payments to specific milestone deliveries in the project. They will want to take as much risk as possible out of the project and hold you accountable at each stage. They may want to negotiate license fee refund scenarios as well as your fees for each aspect of the project.

Your objectives in negotiating your financial proposal will include balancing up-front payments against on-going recurring income, avoiding unnecessary risks on delivery and ensuring that the contract satisfies your accounting and legal requirement.

As a general guideline, and obvious as they might seem, examine each negotiating point twice for the following:

- Is there anything in the agreement that might prevent you from recognising your license fee income as it is paid? For example, refund scenarios, conditional acceptance etc...

- Do you have full control over each deliverable without any dependencies on external parties? If not, are the external party deliverables accounted for in your payment plan? For example, if the prospect or a third party must provide you with requirements definitions, the countdown to your time-based deliverable must only commence after it has been delivered.

- Do you have a free rein to license your software elsewhere or are there restrictions being placed on you that could affect your future income? Have you accounted for this in your license fee or elsewhere?

- Is your customer's acceptance process clear and tied down to time limits, i.e. must they accept or reject with stated reason within a finite time of receiving the deliverable? Are you running the risk of having delivered but not being paid until eventual acceptance, if ever?

- Are license fee payments specified in percentages and / or time terms? For example, is your payment amount, method and timing clear upon signature and upon first and subsequent deliverables?

- Have you agreed advance or retrospective payment for your team?

- Have you agreed expense amounts, how they will be claimed and paid? Are there maximums agreed?

- Have you agreed the timing and sequence of the Statements of Work against which you will be paid?

- If the project is international, have you considered the exchange rate risk you are prepared to take? Have you bought forward to cover the risk or have you reached agreement with the prospect to modify your price if the rate varies by more than an agreed percentage?

There will always be specific issues that your agreement will include that cannot be pre-empted here. Remember though, that the key things to avoid are covered at the beginning of this chapter.

Lawyers

Choose a commercial lawyer with specific experience in software license and service agreements and intellectual property rights retention. They may cost you $30,000 to $50,000 on a single contract, but in my opinion, they're worth it! There is sufficient meat in these agreements that, having a lawyer that is capable of quickly sifting through the fat to get to the bone is worth a lot in terms of both time and outcome.

A good lawyer can take the mystery out of not only what is included in the MSA, but what is excluded from it. There are a number of companies that I am aware of that believed they only needed to have their lawyer look over the final draft to ensure that they weren't "exposed" in any way! This is a mistake. From the moment you are engaged in final contract negotiation, involve your lawyer.

In situations where a giant corporation elects to negotiate a MSA with a small business because of the specialist nature of its expertise, it is not unheard of that the prospect would agree to pick up the legal bill for the small business! Yes, you read that correctly! Make the request in advance. They know that the amount involved can be a major disincentive, especially when at that time, there is no guarantee of a contract. If your request fails initially, through perseverance, you may be able to get agreement that they would pay an amount over a particular maximum fee if it is exceeded.

CHAPTER 7

Ten Ways to Continue Your Ascent of the Buyer's Value Chain

Substantially, moving up the buyer's value chain in a significant way comes down to changing your perspective on what was once taken as assumed. The "buyer's value chain" literally means increasing your value to the buyer, and therefore increasing the level of your contribution to the project.

A key objective is to bring your prospect to an awareness of their own costs of fulfilling *assumed* parts of the project. These costs will have been taken for granted on the basis of either;

- no perceived alternative being available, or

- a misplaced belief that some parts of the project are too sensitive to be outsourced.

Your task is to provide your prospect with not only credible, realistic and beneficial alternatives, but to make it clear that it is highly advisable to pursue them. Even in the second case above, whilst some areas of a project may indeed be too sensitive to outsource, most are not.

At certain times throughout your pre-sale process, proposing one or more of the ideas presented in this chapter will be natural progressions from your prospective customer dialogue. At other times, you will need to create opportunities to raise them without the danger of immediate dismissal. Remember that anything that breaks with tradition is often quickly dismissed on the basis that if it was a good idea, it would have been done before!

A few pre-requisites to igniting the rockets that will get you past the event horizon and beyond the point of no return:

- You want to do it. This is going to be tough, challenging and sustained. It is a strategic decision to incur the risks as well as the rewards. The time draw on you personally will be major initially.

- You are determined to step up to the new mark of expectation that will fall upon your company - deal with new levels of responsibility, accountability, risk and reward.

- You are prepared to make the required changes. You already have on board, have access to, or can attract the quantity and calibre of people that can meet the project requirements head-on.

- You are prepared to put in place whatever new systems, quality standards, security compliance or procedures necessary to meet this project and future project criteria.

- You believe that the right thing for your company to do is to expand its service capability to the required degree (which you determine).

You've got the pre-requisites in place? Get ready then to start your mind-storming process. Use these ten ideas both as they stand, and as a trigger for new, related and unrelated ideas that you will use to get your rocket in the air! I have no doubt that you will be able to add to this list once you start thinking in the certain way that underpins these ideas. That certain way never strays from increasing your value contribution in the overall project, improving your service to your customer and growing the net worth of your company.

One: License Your Roadmap by Selling Your Vision first

An excellent way to significantly move up the value chain is to view what you have today as phase one of the rollout of your complete vision. There is a good probability that what you have today is part of a wider solution concept with a bigger value benefit to your customer.

Sell your *vision* as the primary value proposition. This contrasts with the traditional way of selling which is to sell what you have today as part of your vision. See the difference? The first stage in the project will be the implementation of your current solution and you will agree subsequent steps to be implemented and when.

This of course sounds too easy when stated in a single paragraph as above. But think about it for a moment. There can be several reasons why a customer may prefer to license your future roadmap instead of just what you have today. Some of these reasons are:

- They have a substantially bigger economic benefit, either through cost saving or profit improvement.

- You have given them an opportunity to work with you to influence the design of your standard development roadmap in their favour. They will get things that they would otherwise not be in a position to get – from any vendor.

- They may be offered a time-based competitive advantage against their competition by having early access to your roadmap releases as beta and even alpha testers.

- You have agreed, as part of the engagement to additionally develop some (paid for) bespoke elements of the project which, if integrated at design stage during the development of your standard roadmap, can yield significant advantage to your prospect.

- As part of the deal, based on its overall size and duration, you may agree to locate a team from your company in the physical offices of your prospect (or nearby) to facilitate knowledge transfer and successful execution of the project.

- As part of an engagement of this size, you have agreed to assign your top people to the project who will work hand in glove with the customer's team.

Gaining prospect buy-in to your vision alone can treble or quintuple the value of your proposed solution. To attain it, not only must your vision have credibility and be aligned with the prospect's goal, but you must prove that you have the ability to deliver on that vision.

Nothing serves this purpose better than to produce working "walkthroughs" of your vision such as HTML front-end prototypes. This allows the prospect to visualize exactly what you mean, shows that you have thought this through and demonstrates a certain credibility that you can deliver on it. Even though there is no actual working functionality underneath the front-end, the walkthrough allows you to show your prospect things that can "blow them away"! Of course, the challenge is up to you to subsequently deliver on it.

Remember that these HTML walkthroughs take relatively little time to produce and contribute massively to perceived value creation. Before you build them, make sure you have an excellent understanding of what your prospect would "love to have", "dreams about" or would pay a lot of money for! This truly is a unique opportunity to create massive value and establish excellent credibility!

A Few further notes

When you have achieved prospect buy-in to your roadmap, your goal is to arrive at an overall license fee inclusive of all existing and future software elements or modules described in your specifications. Payment of your license fee, howsoever structured in your MSA, should proportionately consider your base system or core architecture, initially agreed functionality to be deployed (currently available), and individual functional elements as they become available. Better still, negotiate sequenced percentage payments of your license fee based on specific stages of your roadmap being completed. Where particular prospect requirements are being incorporated into roadmap components, it is fair and reasonable to negotiate these payments.

Finally, put a functional and time-based limitation on your roadmap. You will very probably find that neither you nor your prospective customer considers it practical to license a future roadmap beyond three years. This is good! By placing a functional boundary on your roadmap, you are preserving the option to additionally license to the customer new functionality that may be conceived and developed during the course of the project – for example, for other customers!

Also, a time boundary is the point at which you can once again engage your customer on a big scale. One of your objectives throughout the course of the current project will be to identify the next big ticket opportunity that comes in three years time! A year into your project when you are so absorbed into its detail, this can be surprisingly easy to forget.

Two: Expand the Scope of Your Outsourced Solution

Prospects can often be taken by complete surprise when they discover that a new alternative to something that they have assumed had no alternatives, surfaces. Usually these are pleasant surprises. At worst, they do no damage to your proposal. At best, you get asked how exactly you would propose to do whatever it is you have proposed.

For example, if your software is to be deployed in an internal Data Centre within the prospect's organization, you might have proposed that you undertake the prime contract to deploy, host and manage the solution in a secure external hosting environment instead of the prospect's own Data Centre. You may have proposed that you additionally undertake responsibility for a second Continuity of Business (CoB) site with a specified switchover period or a portfolio of management services to report on real time performance and support issues.

Your expanded proposal must obviously be an extension of your solution that you welcome. It is a proactive suggestion from you that your company, either alone or in partnership with another vendor, can significantly improve on your overall value contribution to the project.

In making your expanded proposal, your intention is to enable your prospect to revisit its reasons for either wanting to do it in-house, inviting other companies to bid on that part of the project or for not having invited you to bid on it in the first place. You would be amazed at the number of times that a prospect will assume that you are either not interested or unable to bid for certain parts of a project, without ever having asked you!

What you are looking for here and what you are hoping your prospect may discover is:

- that nothing other than existing structures and processes are suggesting that they should be doing it in-house.

- that these structures and processes, upon deeper analysis, were inherited and enforced by older technologies and are now obsolete, and that significant cost economies can be attained by outsourcing it.

- that it is desirable to have the least number of vendors possible to be involved in the project such that, when a problem arises, accountability is centralized.

- that your solution actually provides less risk to the prospect than doing it in-house. (You will of course have rationalized this!)

- . . . and that your company is visibly looking for new ways of increasing your value to the prospect – something they will appreciate.

Finally, when you look for ways to expand the extent and direction of your proposal, look for opportunities to build on both the functional scope of the project as well as the extent of the services you provide.

Three: Align to Your Prospect's Value Metrics

Are you crystal clear on how your prospect will measure the success of this project? Do you know exactly how your prospect will value your solution? Is there a percentage relationship between these two answers?

If you're like most (but not all) software companies, the answer is very probably not. Even though you may never succeed in fully and exactly aligning them, your resolute and unwavering efforts to do so significantly help your goal of building perceived value.

A prospect may develop a perceived value of your solution based on several factors including

- Your on-going early-stage, pre-proposal discussion on license fees

- The financial proposal in your RFP response

- Your Competitor's financial proposal – even though it is extremely rare and unlikely that a like-with-like comparison can be made.

- The entire professional "aura" surrounding your company – the degree of quality it portrays

- The very size and nature of your company.

Whilst the natural tendency is towards these factors in establishing a value for your products and services, they nevertheless ignore the real value to the customer of successfully delivering on the project's goals. These project goals may be

i.   To phase out an existing solution which may be costing millions of dollars annually to maintain.

ii.   To maintain a competitive position that is
      presently being eroded at a rate of millions of
      dollars per year.

iii. To recover lost competitive ground that may
      have already cost millions of dollars.

iv.   To deliver its services to its served market for a
      cost that is less than half of what it costs today.

v.   To reduce administration and management
      overhead by eliminating the need for manual
      processes.

So there is clearly a very great gap that naturally arises
between these two value points. What do you do? You
precede your financial proposal by doing the research
you know you should have done in all your previous
prospect proposals – but didn't do (!). You find out what
exactly these project success metrics are, how they are
measured, who measures them, over what period of
time are they calculated and understand how your
solution uniquely contributes to the attainment of the
desired results.

All your subsequent early, middle and late stage
dialogue on commercial issues should always relate to

the economic benefit attained. If you can, make proposals that "risk-share" with the prospect – a percentage down plus a percentage based on economic benefit attained. If you can, link your pricing model to attained benefit. Try to avoid a finger-in-the-air pricing method and definitely do not link your price to either your costs or your historical "list price" if one exists.

Obvious as this might seem, what you are doing is bringing home the actual value of success at every opportunity. You are setting an expectation that allows your prospect to, sometimes uncomfortably, pre-empt what will be contained in your financial proposal. But you are doing it in a way that, from your point of view, is good for them and good for you. More often than most, if your prospect's expectation is such that they believe it is going to create a problem for you when it comes to proposal short-listing – take a cue from them and probe what ball-park you need to be in.

Irrespective of what is in your financial proposal, you know that you will be heavily negotiated on a big ticket sale. They will fight it on the basis that their economic benefit is not your business – but of course, it is. The converse is that your cost base is not their business. Wouldn't you rather be negotiated from $8m down to $5m than from $800K down to $500K?

Four: Get Recognition for Your Architecture and Data Model

A significant proportion of your intellectual property in the solution may well be contained in the design of your architecture and your data model. This is especially so in enterprise applications which deal with third parties both in consumer and business markets.

I gave you a caution earlier in the book *not* to release these designs during the pre-sale process, despite the certainty that they will be asked for. Believe it or not, many companies make the mistake of readily, and often coyly handing over these designs. By doing do, they risk their designs being emulated by an unscrupulous prospect (yes, sometimes they exist!), or even finding their way into a competitor's hands. This can occur through a disgruntled employee leaving your prospect, joining your competitor and literally stealing as much intellectual content as they can lay their hands on.

No amount of non-disclosure agreements can prevent this – despite the onus being on the prospect to ensure that this does not happen. Even though the risks to the prospect may be great, it can be an arduous task to prove a case.

So, why take and be seen to be taking, as many precautions as possible to protect your architecture and data model? The answer is because they are very, very valuable. Treating them as being very valuable and getting value recognition for them however are different challenges!

In a nutshell, the value recognition you should be targeting to get for your architecture and data model, is their *future contribution* to the overall solution. Unto themselves, they hold no functional value for your prospect, so this can be a tough part of your negotiation. Their contribution to the future solution however, may be that they allow future functionality to be implemented more easily, that they allow performance levels to be maintained despite massive increases in user volumes, that they allow complex data structures to be implemented or that they allow multi-channel solution delivery based on a single view of the customer.

Even when you get *conceptual* value recognition here, it is unlikely that your prospect is going to be able to put an actual monetary amount on the "intangible".

Here are two ways you can use to gain monetary value for your architecture and data model:

1) Incorporate your architecture and data model license fee in the overall license fee for your "base" system. In other words:

   Base System License Fee =
   Existing Functionality, plus Architecture +
   Data Model.

2) Get recognition in terms of its percentage contribution to overall "fit" against the customer requirement. In other words, as you revisit the complete requirements list, identify particular capabilities that can be delivered in present and future production releases as a result of the architecture and data model, i.e. a front-end only is needed.

   What you are moving towards here is, if the total software license for the solution over three years is $5m, your existing functionality represents approximately 20% of the required functionality and your architecture and data model represents a mutually agreed estimate of an additional 15%. In this case, your architecture is valued at $750,000.

In case "2" above, you should be aiming to get paid for your architecture during the first project phase. Your prospect may argue that they will not be able to fully use your architecture until you have developed all the remaining functionality they will need. Your counter argument is that, nevertheless you will be delivering the complete architecture during phase one implementation and, because of this, the prospect will be able to deploy future phases in a more secure or easier way.

Five: Separate Maintenance from Support

It amuses me that the software industry, being perceived as so "hi-tech", still allows itself to be a prisoner of tradition. It is as slow to change as many of the industries it often gripes about for not changing quickly enough so that they need new software!

One of those traditions relates to older generations of software which used to be sold as a "big bang" license fee with a percentage of the license fee – often 15% - 21% being payable annually thereafter as "maintenance and support"! Not only does this model not work anymore, the customer *paradigm* has changed. What this means is that internet service delivery now demands 24x7 support capability, guaranteed up-time and performance levels in your customer's Service Level Agreement (SLA), electronic and people based support infrastructure, full pre-production testing on mirror sites before moving to a new release and so on. The issue of maintenance and support has become so huge in itself that it is rarely appreciated even among customers, what the full implications of this paradigm shift actually are.

The bottom line is that the individual services of "maintenance" and "support" have become so critical that you should no longer treat them as a single solution.

There was a time when the customer support organization used to be able to comfortably handle the deployment of new software releases. This is not so any more. The "Mega" applications have become too complex. Even their testing and quality assurance processes now demand much more structure and formality than ever before. Pre-production testing and production deployment may often now require input from Database Administrators, Development Engineering as well as QA and Production Control.

The fundamental split between maintenance and support can be summarized as:

Maintenance

This is the service you will provide to keep your customer's application at the latest revision level. It may involve updates, upgrades and, if you're an Application Service Provider, production control services, disaster recovery and continuity of business services.

Support

This is your person to person help desk, electronic service and, if provided, on-site assistance for your customer. Three levels of support service are generally recognized.

> **Level 1** usually refers to an "end user" support service of logging calls and addressing basic end user issues. For example, if you sell an on-line Bill Payments solution to a Utility service provider, the "end user" in this instance is the consumer. However the Utility provider itself may prefer to directly provide Level 1 support to its end users. Alternatively of course, there is nothing stopping you from proposing that you provide a full Level 1 service to their customers on their behalf, if that's what you want to do – and many do.

Level 2 typically refers to a good degree of application proficiency and may either feed into Level 1 or communicate directly with the end user. In most cases, Level 2 will be a service provided by you to your customer. This will be the case at least initially. A customer may wish to build its own competency at Level 2.

Level 3 requires detailed technical proficiency in the solution at all levels from design to service delivery. In your case, Level 3 should have full access to your development team and will be a high value service to your customer.

What all of this adds up to is that your maintenance and support services should be quoted for separately. In cases where a 24x7 support service is required, the figures can add up very substantially. You may agree with your customer for example, that a Level 3 service must be provided 24x7 by two people dedicated to this customer alone. That's six "Full Time Equivalents" (FTE) – two people on three eight hour work shifts. But level three is highly specialist and skilled, so the cost to you per FTE is going to be say, $120,000 before other costs.

Multiply that by six and you have your *before profit* figure of $720,000 annually for a Level 3 support service alone.

Six: Separate Updates from Upgrades

The software industry seems to be catching onto this one as it can be seen more and more often. A clear distinction between "updates" and "upgrades" is drawn.

Updates

Always included in a standard maintenance agreement, updates are on-going bug-fixes and improvements to the core licensed software. These are the software maintenance releases that a customer expects to resolve known bugs, improve performance, refine a clumsy front end etc...

Upgrades

Upgrades are functional enhancements to licensed software which build upon declared functionality. This additional functionality is likely to not have been available at the time of contract but subsequently became available as time progressed.

An "upgrade" opportunity can arise in several situations. Some examples are:

- Functionality developed for one customer is desired to be incorporated into the environment of another. Of course, you have negotiated the intellectual property rights to do this!

- You identified and speculatively developed new functionality that was not specified in your MSA, but your customer would now like to have it.

- You acquired another software solution and incorporated it into your application.

If you've negotiated your intellectual property rights on funded development (see previous chapter), licensing upgrades can be a very viable and lucrative way to increase your added value to your customer. When the functional enhancement is big enough – for example, an entirely new module, and if your customer wants it, you have a captive audience!

In some cases, where joint development is involved, you can even trade functionality with your customer. This may not always be practical.

Seven: Guarantee Your Share of Development

For the purpose of this idea, let's assume that the big-ticket project you are negotiating involves a substantial customization or bespoke development effort. Let's also assume that either:

- In pursuit of its key goal for knowledge transfer during the project, your prospect is intent on developing as much as possible of the bespoke software in-house. This is not unreasonable and regularly occurs, or

- Your prospect intends to subcontract a significant proportion of the work to another third party who may be its incumbent developer of software.

Necessarily, you will be involved in the development project as much of the expertise and domain know-how resides with you. Additionally, you need to be involved when integration with your core system is needed.

However, you might find this situation somewhat uncomfortable, despite the fact that the prospect's intention is honourable and the expectation from you is reasonable. You're uncomfortable for a few particular reasons:

- Use of your company's resource in this way is almost purely as a body shop. But you're not a body shop. You know that you can achieve significantly greater turnover on your people asset by employing them on work that results in future products.

- Loss of control. You know that, unless your employees are the driving force in the specific development work taking place, you will most likely have to contend with more misunderstandings, longer lead times, less influence on what will be developed, and reduced executive control on the project.

- Reduced scope for the acquisition and reuse of intellectual property. It is very hard indeed to acquire deep understanding of something when no real time or incentive exists on the prospect side to make sure you understand what they developed.

This can mean millions of dollars, yet you see your role reducing and reducing. You can even see a situation arising where you are relegated to "consultant" on the project and being forced back to an advisory capacity when needed.

Instead of falling back into second place behind the prospect's or a third party's development team, recognize that you are in a strong position *pre-contract* to negotiate a minimum percentage of the overall development effort and funds being placed on you. 50% or more is not unreasonable assuming that you show and demonstrate your ability to provide the required resource.

Your bid for a minimum percentage of the development spend is sustainable because:

- You have now or are committed to putting in place the required resource.

- You very reasonably want to restrict access to your source code to your prospect's organization and do not wish it to be accessed by any third party. For all you know, despite their best intentions now, you could be competing with this third party at any time in the future. Additionally, someone could leave the third party's employment and carry with them an in-depth understanding of your work. These are very good reasons to sway your prospect to your way of thinking when it comes to intellectual property release.

- The rate sheet you are negotiating as part of the MSA reflects this volume of work. If this work is not placed on you before a specified and agreed cut-off date in the MSA, the prospect should be contractually obliged to pay you any outstanding balance between the dollar amount of the volume of work committed to and the amount actually placed.

- You are best positioned to undertake this work in the first place.

Conversely, from the prospect's perspective, if you commit to putting in place the resource needed to deliver the project, your failure to do so within an agreed timeframe, should allow your prospect to involve a third party.

Eight: Merger or Acquisition – Don't Concede the License!

It seems we never really consider that the very dramatic may actually happen! It often does. Retrospectively, we forgive ourselves with self-talk like "the odds were against it", "it probably would not have happened" etc...

Mergers and acquisitions (M&A) do happen, have always been popular and can strike anywhere, anytime and with organizations of every size. So this is your heads-up. This is your warning that, should you concede on the M&A issue again, when it happens, you will know that you could have been so, so much wealthier! What am I talking about? Here's the situation.

Fast-forward one, two or three years into the future. Irrespective of whether your customer was acquired, acquired another organization or merged with another company, the combined entity is going to be faced with a decision. Does the enlarged organization roll out your solution across the entirety of its new population? Does it dump your solution and roll out the other organization's solution? Or does it remain separate and proceed as two halves of a whole?

We know the last is not a realistic option in the medium term and possibly not in the short term either. The odds are therefore at least 50/50 that your solution will be chosen. Better if you are leading the field.

At the time of negotiating your MSA, your prospect is fully aware of the implications here. Despite the fact that a merger or acquisition might be imminent, whether known or unknown to the people you are dealing with, your prospect will expect you to accept a clause under the authorities of their rights to use your software, that gives them free rein to roll out your software, at no additional cost to all of its "affiliate" companies, past or future, as it may deem appropriate. Subtle isn't it?

You should adopt a tactical position on this. Allow the right to use the software at all *existing, declared* affiliates. The prospect must provide a list as an inclusion within the MSA. Agree also that the rights of future affiliates to use your software at no fee will not be *unreasonably withheld.* State clearly that, in the event of a merger or acquisition, whereby the combined organization exceeds the size of the current organization by say, 25% or greater, an additional license fee is payable in direct proportion to the enlarged organization.

That's a bit of mouthful. But have another read. It means that such an event is a potential deal doubler for you! Should your prospect be either acquired or merged, it is likely that the other organization is also a very big fish – putting you into an interesting position if yours is the preferred solution!

It will be interesting for you to observe your prospect's reaction to your negotiating position on this. You may be able to read something from it. If they fight it hard, it is reasonable for you to assume that they know something that you don't! The best possible situation of course, is that they lodge a token objection but concede it nevertheless. A really interesting situation is where they have conceded it but come back at the next opportunity and try to renegotiate it! A behind-the-scenes reviewer exists.

The M&A issue can be worth nothing or millions of dollars. If you're still in play when the agreement is signed, you could potentially make a killing for no effort!

Nine: Agree to Exclusivity – But Price it into Planetary Orbit!

Many companies make the post-RFP short-list because they agreed to the possibility of an exclusive license for their software. Conversely, many more companies did not make the shortlist because they refused to entertain the idea!

Who do you think made the right decision? In all circumstances, companies in the first scenario prevail. They are right because they *entertained discussion* of the *possibility* of entering an exclusive arrangement with the prospect. No commercial conditions surrounding such exclusivity have yet been discussed, let alone agreed. Their commercial proposal in their RFP response outlined a licensing scenario or scenarios, which was non-exclusive, but they showed a *willingness* to engage on an exclusive basis.

This might seem pedantic or even trivial, but when you consider the small percentage of engagements that start out with exclusivity as a demand, which actually end up exclusive, the issue can be viewed as substantially tactical on the prospect's part. So how do you counter this and how can "non-exclusivity" move you *up* the value chain?

I confess that I have not always played this one exactly right. But on the occasions when I have had most success, I can make a few retrospective observations:

Pricing an exclusive license can actually support the value of a non-exclusive license! For example, if you price your exclusive license at say $30m for a three year period within a particular geography, a $5 million fee for a perpetual, non-exclusive license would appear somewhat more interesting. Especially so when you can fully rationalize and support your $30m price tag by convincing your prospect that you realistically expect to write up at least six non-exclusive deals of similar size within three years!

When you price for exclusivity, you are pricing to offset lost opportunity which can be absolutely massive. You are being "bought out" of a market that you have forecasted sales against, and compensation would need not only to reflect this but to reward you for potential growth that you would likely have found through your activities in that market.

Anti-monopoly and pro-competition legislation across the entire globe has actually placed genuine restrictions on organizations' ability to strike exclusive arrangements that preclude others. Your prospect knows this well, but also knows that even if they were found guilty of having one, the only reprimand would most likely be to cease and desist! And they would already have acquired a major time advantage against their competition!

Nevertheless, price high enough, be credible, show reasonable rationale and your prospect will veer away from exclusivity.

Big fish are very protective when it comes to their markets and their competitive position in those markets. If they cannot get exclusivity from you at reasonable cost, then they will set out to build as much protection for themselves in the MSA as you are prepared to concede. I firmly believe that this is the real reason why the exclusivity issue is ever raised in the first place.

In the absence of exclusivity, your prospect may want:

- A defined time period within which you agree not to engage one of its competitors – say six months.

- A project plan that totally absorbs what it considers to be your best people for as long as possible. This of course locks out their competition by stealth.

- "Preferred customer" status from you which guarantees that you will not sell to another customer for a lower price.

- Advance access to new functionality as it becomes available before it enters general market release.

All of the above customer safeguards build your value for the prospect and further support your non-exclusive license fee at your proposed level. Do not forget that, irrespective of what your proposed non-exclusive license level was, it will always be negotiated

downwards. There are no exceptions. Your final
negotiated resting place is significantly influenced by
your ability to support your license fee.

So put your exclusive license fee into planetary orbit and
be willing to negotiate certain compensating safeguards
in exchange for agreement on your non-exclusive
license fee. If you really need to go to the nth degree,
you can actually put a monetary value on each of the
four safeguards above.

Ten: Get and Keep an Executive Role in the Project

In "seven", I wrote about your need to assert your
position in the project and get a guaranteed percentage
of the development spend. In an overall project context,
your post-engagement role is less something that you
negotiate per se, but more something that you mutually
agree with the prospect as being in the best interests of
the project. Nevertheless, the various roles which your
individual team members will play can significantly
impact your future income from the project.

You should be sufficiently confident and capable of
promoting specific individuals in your team as team
leaders, group leaders, sub-project managers, even joint

project manager or project director, in addition to designers, analysts, programmers, testers etc...

Consider aiming for:

- A sufficient influence, if not control, on the direction of the project. In particular, you need assurance that the project maintains focus on general market demands rather than steering too far towards a specific end user demand; a major pitfall in projects designed for commercial end users.

- A position that allows you to inject sometimes large doses of reality - effectively. These reality doses will often have to do with what can be delivered and when. Remember that you are a software company used to product delivery deadlines where sometimes it is more important to make a limited release than to make no release at all. Your prospect's organization is very likely not to be used to this kind of pressured project delivery to the same degree you are. You can only maintain expectations based on reality if you have an executive presence.

- Positions within the business analysis team that can keep the focus on real end user priorities instead of too much detail in small areas.

Positions in the I.T. team that ensure first hand, things like site preparation, deployment processes and procedures are adhered to. Positions in the development team including functional specification and design, coding, front-end, database design and positions in the Q.A. team to ensure deliverables are tested and accepted as agreed.

- A project management role that is continually ready and willing to approach and be approached on delicate matters.

So how do these roles influence your income from the project? Apart from the obvious reason – to keep it flowing, your team's vantage point to spot and act on new opportunities as they arise can not only improve your income but can be of major service to your customer.

What your customer gets that was not explicitly procured in the MSA, is an abundance of highly experienced and highly qualified external inputs. These are intellectual and experience based inputs into its existing systems, processes, procedures, customer requirements and even its wider market and competitive position. It is a completely new and very substantial source of new ideas and opportunities that could never realistically have been provided by its own staff. This is worth thinking about.

To stand the best chance of actually identifying and credibly feeding back these new ideas and opportunities to your prospect, your front-end in this respect is the good people you have placed in key project positions. The opportunity to do this for both yourself and your customer is so significant that it once again places a major highlight on the need to gain senior and executive presence at all levels of the project.

Managed well, an "awareness" of the inevitability of lurking opportunity, will keep you moving up your buyer's value chain long after your initial engagement.

Bonus Tip #11: Keep Your Eyes Peeled

Keep your eyes peeled on every piece of draft documentation, either commercial or technical, which comes in from your prospect pre-contract. These include things like draft term sheets, sample agreements, sample attachments, statements of work, addendums, forms etc...

You would be truly amazed at the number of times that a piece of information escapes into one of these documents that you were never supposed to see. It can happen either by accident or slipped through "accidentally on purpose" by a friendly contact who may never be able to acknowledge it! Little pieces of information like this can often reveal:

- A serious competitive weakness that you can capitalize on.
- A maximum budget allowance on a particular aspect of the project.
- An undeleted comment from a hidden reviewer that revealed your prospect's intention.
- A willingness to concede on a major aspect of the negotiation in exchange for something that you can concede easily.
- A date by which a budget must be spent!
- A premature instruction to someone in your prospect organization, relating to launching their new solution (yours) in the open market!
- A personal comment!

These are just a handful of the real-life "messages" which escaped the prospect's net. At the respective times and in the respective projects, every single one potentially turned the deal. I still believe they were accidental though!

CHAPTER 8

Wrap-Up: A Few Tens

You've now completed *Selling High Value Software*. So how did you get on? Were you able to visualize yourself and your team doing these things? Did you consider all or any of the ideas and negotiating strategies realistic? I hope you did. Because, if you did, there is a good chance that you will make at least one, and potentially a number, of adjustments to your activities or thinking that you may not otherwise have made. If you have, you are about to enter a realm that will energize you not just with reinvigorated ambition, but with a new commitment to locate and engage these projects and the challenges that ensue.

This final chapter is structured in "tens" so that lots of information can be summarized or bulleted in a relatively small space. I'm OK about this because the purpose of the *bullets* is to get you thinking about them – not to give you *all* the answers! It is you that should be considering these issues or answering these questions and raising new ones for yourself. I've also been advised to keep my book in or around the two hundred page mark so that it is both readable and will be read. I've therefore purposely presented this information in the form of "tens" so as not to dilute the main purpose of the book which maintains a very specific focus on *Selling High Value Software*.

So here is the chapter of "tens" that is designed to stretch you – just a bit, and generally get you into *big picture review mode* so that you can set the stage for what lies ahead. Don't worry if I cheat a little and combine a few questions into one!

Before we get you really thinking, let's start with the most logical follow-on – your post-sale.

Ten Things You Can Do To Maintain Momentum Post Sale

When you've engaged the project, here are a few things to do and look out for as your project progresses. Some are very obvious, some you will be pulled into by your customer and some require your initiative. They're all important.

i.   Manage your "face time" and that of your team. Relationships cannot be built at a distance. Regular face-to-face contact cannot be replaced.

ii.   Deliver on time. If you anticipate a problem with meeting a delivery deadline, give plenty of notice, manage expectations early, set a new deadline and meet it.

iii.   Deliver excellent quality in every respect –
never compromise, always exceed
expectations.

iv.   If you are working at distance, pre-schedule
individual team conference calls at least weekly.
Enforce a discipline in your team of advance
preparation. Develop excellent conference call
etiquette.

v.   Be innovative – stay idea-driven.

vi.   Keep the political status quo – solve problems
at the level at which they arise.

vii.   Assert your position in the project. Leverage
your company's experience. You are experts at
what can be realistically delivered and when.
Speak up if the project is going on a tangent.
Highlight lower priority or limited market
requirements. Keep the focus on high-return
activity and release functionality. Keep the
pressure positive!

viii.   Publicly give credit where credit is due.

ix.   Hold regular one-to-one 'phone calls between
the more formal, scheduled conference calls,

with *each of* the key individuals in your customer's project team. Stay friendly and approachable. Be the one to call or be called if there's a problem.

x.   Hold executive face-to-face project review meetings at least bi-monthly initially unless scheduled more frequently.

Ten Basic Things About Your Team to Check

If there is a single one of these missing, you need to take action to resolve it – whatever it takes. No excuses.

i.   Your sales team uses a proven selling *system* such as Sandler, Miller-Heiman or Carnegie. I'm not referring to selling techniques or sales process automation, both of which are also important. I'm referring to an actual "system" in which your sales team is trained, periodically updated and which is consistently practiced.

ii.   Your marketing activities are direct response focused – not image or brand focused. Some might disagree with me here, but I'm a firm believer in rifle-shot targeting rather than the big crowd pleaser!

iii. You have built your business on the back of excellent customer relationships. You enjoy the trust and respect of your customers and take a personal interest in serving them. If you are the CEO, you personally meet your top ten customers at least twice per year.

iv. You have an effective, process-driven prospecting system and plan in situ that is in perpetual motion to fill your sales pipeline.

v. You employ only excellent sales professionals who can articulate big ticket value propositions and can build relationships at senior executive level.

vi. You network in the right places because you enjoy it and are good at it – not because you feel you have to. If you're not good at it, get someone else to do it for you.

vii. You sell customer benefits and return on investment – not features and technology.

viii. You have maintained a spirit and culture of entrepreneurship in your team. You have not sat back just because you managed to get a business up and running.

ix. You are proud of your management team and trust every single one of them to step up to the mark in the mega-deal.

x. You have organized your business to allow you to spend a significant percentage of your time growing it, while your trusted team manages it.

Ten Things To Explore With Your Customer At Your Next Meeting

Make sure you are talking to your customer contacts at the right level. Talk to people who set strategy such as senior executives, CIO's, CFO's, CPO's and better still, CEO's. Talk to several people if you can.

i. The top three issues that your customer excels at that keeps its business strong in the marketplace.

ii. The single unique selling proposition it leverages in its served market and why its customers see it as being so important.

iii.   Your customer's vision of how its industry will evolve over the next three to five years. What changes lie ahead and how will your customer react to those changes?

iv.   Excluding labour, what are the three biggest costs in running your customer's business?

v.   What causes the CEO, COO, CIO and CFO to loose sleep at night?

vi.   What are the highest level three to five year goals that the company has set? What will be the principle determinants in achieving these goals?

vii.   What areas of the business do they think will need to be improved or strengthened in the foreseeable future?

viii.   In ballpark figures, roughly what investment does your customer make each year in maintaining existing information systems as well as deploying new I.T. solutions? When are budgets for this investment set?

ix.   Relating to these investments, how are needs
      prioritised? Are solutions outsourced or
      developed in-house? If in-house, what is the
      rationale for this?

x.   From your customer's perspective, what does it
      see as your own company's strengths and
      weaknesses? How could you serve them
      better?

Ten Questions To Ask Yourself When Re-examining Your Market

Whilst you do need to stand back and take a big picture
view, look first within your immediate market. Then look
in the immediate vicinity of your market; think in terms of
"one step" away. For example, one step away from your
main customer contact (their colleague, their boss, their
Department etc...), one step away from department-
wide deployment (enterprise-wide deployment), one
step away from the problem which your solution solves
(a bigger related problem), one step away from your
geographic market (international market) and so on.
Finally, look at the possibility of new markets that could
be addressed by leveraging the core competencies that
exist within your organization (new or expanded
services, partnerships, channel, joint ventures etc...)

i.   Is this the right market to be in? Is it growing? Can I grow with it? What barriers to growth exist?

ii.   Is my original vision for this industry still valid? If not, have I adapted it? Do I still believe in it heart and soul? Am I actually pursuing it or have I gone off on a tangent?

iii.   Is my value proposition capable of being tweaked, modified or adapted in some way to deliver a clearer or incremental benefit?

iv.   What new lateral or tangential market segments or niches should I be looking at?

v.   Do I show my customers how much I care about them? How? What did I do for them lately that was unexpected? What can I do tomorrow?

vi.   Do my customers like working with my company? Or do they do it because they have no alternative?

vii.   Are there other parts of my customer's organization for which I could build solutions?

viii.   Are there more senior people in my customer's
        organization who could open new doors if I
        could only get to them?

ix.   Is my company doing things now that, had it
      known about previously, would not have started
      them? If so, plan to end them as quickly as
      possible.

x.   What problems do I or could I solve that could
     deliver very significant savings or profit
     improvement for my customers?

Ten Things Your Customers Enjoy!

This is my chance to evangelize a little about the
importance of customer satisfaction and some of the
simple things you can do to promote it! Of course, you'll
uncover more individual ones, but here are a few that
you can be pretty certain about.

i.   They enjoy buying! They may not like being sold
     to, but most people actually like buying things!

ii.   They enjoy saying nice things about you and
      complimenting you. Really – they do! So give
      them lots of reasons to do it!

iii. They enjoy it when a decision pays off. Over-deliver and out-perform, always.

iv. They enjoy being recognized for excellence. Build case studies around them. Have them speak at your seminars. Use their commentary in press editorials etc...

v. They enjoy humour that they appreciate. Don't assume it but it's worth trying to get it right!

vi. They enjoy attention. Listen well. Speak well.

vii. They enjoy it when someone clearly goes out of their way to help them or to do something special for them. Do it regularly and enjoy doing it.

viii. They enjoy success at every level. However it is measured, be a part of the reason for it.

ix. They enjoy achieving things. Be a source of ideas. Help them to achieve. Inspire them to achieve.

x. They enjoy being with people that they trust.

Ten Unacceptably Weak Excuses for Inaction!

Don't let yourself be fooled by fears and doubts. Stand up and be counted at this level. Remember when you arrived at that boat? Your fishing rod had your name engraved on it – and you didn't even know that you owned one! All that's required is your *decision* to do it. Everything can change from there.

    i.   "My market will never pay that amount of money".

        Remember - align to your customer's cost and profit metrics. Find the problem(s) and the customers that will yield big ticket returns on their investment. This is about perceived value.

        You could indeed be stuck in a low ticket value market. There is a reasonable chance however that you have *positioned* yourself in this low ticket segment, but that your existing customers are spending much bigger money with other vendors who may only be one step removed from you. It is also quite possible that the opportunity to re-position yourself may be hampered significantly by your own beliefs. Some creative thinking is clearly needed and this book should have given you some good ideas to explore. However, if you go through the process and still believe you're stuck, you should seriously consider expanding your market on the back of your core competencies. Challenge your entrepreneurship!

ii.   "My competitors ensure that ticket value stays low".

Do not assume that your competitors have got the market definition right either. If you can find the problem with the required return, and solve it, you will leave your competitors far behind. This is not an overnight sortie. It is something you start now and evolve. Avoid *constraining* your creativity by even thinking about your existing competitors. Stay focused on your customer. There is one exception to this! Has your competitor discovered something in the background that you haven't yet seen?

iii.   "My solution just isn't worth that".

Firstly, we are not necessarily talking about your current solution – but we *could* be! We are possibly talking about an evolution of your solution, most probably one step removed or adapted to a different *type* of customer. However, if you believe your solution is not worth more, then you are correct.

iv.　"Licensing my roadmap is too risky".

Some view their roadmap as intellectual content which, if it ever made its way to their competitors, they would be finished! The bottom line is that your roadmap is a pipedream until it is realized. I can think of no better way to realizing it and even improving it, than having its development funded by your customers.

v.　"My company is too small to make it through a MSA due diligence process".

Some of the biggest whales in the ocean seek out that tiny little gourmet meal that no one else can enjoy but them! If a big fish wants what you have, your size will ultimately not stand in the way.

vi.　"My team is already stretched"

Are they stretching for normality and survival or are they stretching for success and growth? Stretch them a bit more – you may find that the trees of survival and success are actually the same height. Only the direction of stretch needs to be changed. Re-examine your team's activities. Be more selective in the work you target and accept.

vii. "My company is not big enough to build a solution with this kind of price tag".

It is. You are building perceived value to solve a problem. Success here is not measured in lines of code.

viii. "I've so much on my plate right now that I cannot afford the time luxury of what you call creative thinking. Especially when there is no guarantee of success".

If you think like this, you're right. Don't waste your time.

ix. "My sales team are not up to it"

Can they be taught or trained? If not, you will need to hire new people for this quest. In the meantime, do it yourself. When you get some traction, you can grow the initiative.

x. "I'm in sales, but my manager will never allow me to spend this amount of effort on 'dream-chasing'!"

Go it alone and do it by stealth. This activity does not need to impact your sales performance. It can be done in parallel. However, do introduce your manager to this book. You will need full buy-in and support from your company once you hook a whale.

Ten Things You Can Do Today That Will Move You to Action

There is not one of these things you cannot or should not do. You cannot be excused for inaction. This is where you will really get the creative juices flowing!

i. *Decide* now to up the ante. Commit to engage the process of creating mega-ticket value.

ii. Immediately, set up individual appointments with your top ten customers, commencing about two weeks hence so that you can prepare to specifically discuss what you are setting out to do.

iii.   Review, refine and articulate your vision *on paper*. Understand exactly how your vision translates to value. A question for you only - How much is your vision worth?

iv.   Review this wrap-up chapter by yourself and then with your team. Consider buying a corporate license for this book and make it mandatory reading for your team – if you would like to do this, please send an email to info@praxisnow.ie and let me know what you need.

v.   Get trained on *Creative Thinking*. Better still; learn a *system* for doing it. Practice it daily until it becomes second nature.

vi.   Examine your sales team – who else should join you on the leading edge of this quest? Are there external parties who could and would be prepared to contribute as part of your *master mind* group?

vii.   Write down any immediate ideas you may have on things to explore further.

viii.   Set and record specific goals in your quest – this month, this quarter and this year.

ix.   Set aside advance, planned time in your diary to do this.

x.   Identify hypothetical partners or sub-contractors you could potentially work with if you were to prime contract an expanded project from one of your customers. What project expansion might be viable? Why would you want to or not want to expand your project responsibilities? (It's often a bad idea. It's the few specific opportunities that are good ideas that you seek). In deciding whether an idea is good or bad, a good starting point is asking whether it fits with your updated vision or not.

That's a wrap!

That's about it. I hope you've been able to glean some value from the book. I've very much enjoyed writing it and wish you every success with your big game fishing expedition!

All the best.

Bibliography

References:

The Sandler Sales Institute, www.sandler.com
Miller Heiman Sales Training, www.millerheiman.com
Dale Carnegie Training, www.dalecarnegie.com
Webex web conferencing, www.webex.com
Microsoft Live Meeting, www.placeware.com
Brian Tracy International, www.briantracy.com

Further recommended reading:

Select Selling, Daly & O'Dea, 2004
Selling The Dream, Kawasaki, 1991
How to be a Rainmaker, Fox, 2003
Becoming a Category of One, Calloway, 2004
Goals!, Tracy, 2003
Lateral Marketing, Kotler and Trias de Bes, 2002
Purple Cow, Godin, 2003
Strategic Partnerships, Wallace, 2004
The Underdog Advantage, Morey and Miller, 2004
ThinkerToys, Michalko, 1991
Why Didn't I Think of That, McCoy, 2002
Breakthrough Thinking, Nadler, 1994
Think and Grow Rich, Hill, 1939
The Five Temptations of a CEO, Lencioni, 1998
The New Strategic Selling, Heiman, Sanchez and Tuleja 2004
Successful Large Account Management, Miller, Heiman Tuleja, 2004
The Seven Habits of Highly Successful People, Covey, 1989
Crossing the Chasm, Moore, 1999
Into the Tornado, Moore, 1998
The Chasm Companion, Wiefels, 2002
The Science of Getting Rich, Wattles, 1910
As a Man Thinketh, Allen, 1906

Email Addresses:

To send a testimonial (which I really appreciate!), enquire about a volume purchase corporate license for *Selling High Value Software,* or to invite me to speak at your next seminar:
info@praxisnow.ie

Profile of John Coburn

John has spent more than twenty years in enterprise software and technology-based sales. Distinguished by many notable international sales successes, John has conducted big-ticket sales contracts across the globe including the USA, Japan, Egypt, Australia and continental Europe.

John held senior executive positions with organizations such as Westinghouse, WBT Systems, Eontec (now Siebel), Mediacom and Deecal International. He has been an executive board member with a number of software and technology-based companies and currently runs his own consulting services and information products business.

A graduate in electronics engineering and marketing, John is a president's club member of the Sandler Sales Institute and lives in Dublin, Ireland.

33397702R00129

Made in the USA
Lexington, KY
24 June 2014